Cambridge Elements

Elements in the Philosophy of Martin Heidegger
edited by
Filippo Casati
Lehigh University
Daniel O. Dahlstrom
Boston University

HEIDEGGER AND HIS PLATONIC CRITICS

Antoine Pageau-St-Hilaire
Boston University and University of Oxford

Shaftesbury Road, Cambridge CB2 8EA, United Kingdom

One Liberty Plaza, 20th Floor, New York, NY 10006, USA

477 Williamstown Road, Port Melbourne, VIC 3207, Australia

314–321, 3rd Floor, Plot 3, Splendor Forum, Jasola District Centre, New Delhi – 110025, India

103 Penang Road, #05–06/07, Visioncrest Commercial, Singapore 238467

Cambridge University Press is part of Cambridge University Press & Assessment, a department of the University of Cambridge.

We share the University's mission to contribute to society through the pursuit of education, learning and research at the highest international levels of excellence.

www.cambridge.org
Information on this title: www.cambridge.org/9781009582520

DOI: 10.1017/9781009582513

© Antoine Pageau-St-Hilaire 2025

This publication is in copyright. Subject to statutory exception and to the provisions of relevant collective licensing agreements, no reproduction of any part may take place without the written permission of Cambridge University Press & Assessment.

When citing this work, please include a reference to the DOI 10.1017/9781009582513

First published 2025

A catalogue record for this publication is available from the British Library

ISBN 978-1-009-58252-0 Hardback
ISBN 978-1-009-58249-0 Paperback
ISSN 2976-5668 (online)
ISSN 2976-565X (print)

Cambridge University Press & Assessment has no responsibility for the persistence or accuracy of URLs for external or third-party internet websites referred to in this publication and does not guarantee that any content on such websites is, or will remain, accurate or appropriate.

Heidegger and His Platonic Critics

Elements in the Philosophy of Martin Heidegger

DOI: 10.1017/9781009582513
First published online: April 2025

Antoine Pageau-St-Hilaire
Boston University and University of Oxford

Author for correspondence: Antoine Pageau-St-Hilaire, apsh@bu.edu

Abstract: This Element introduces the arguments of three prominent Platonic critics of Heidegger – Leo Strauss (1899–1973), Hans-Georg Gadamer (1900–2002), and Jan Patočka (1907–77) – with the aim of evaluating the trenchancy of their criticisms. The Element shows that these three thinkers uncover novel ways of reading Plato nonmetaphysically (where metaphysics is understood in the Heideggerian sense) and thus of undermining Heidegger's narrative concerning Platonism as metaphysics and metaphysics as Platonism. In their readings of the Platonic dialogues, Plato emerges as a proto-phenomenologist whose attention to the ethical-political facticity of human beings leads to the acknowledgment of human finitude and of the fundamental elusiveness of Being. These Platonic critics of Heidegger thus invite us to see in the dialogues a lucid presentation of philosophic questioning rather than the beginning of distorting doctrinal teachings.

Keywords: Martin Heidegger, Plato, Leo Strauss, Hans-Georg Gadamer, Jan Patočka

© Antoine Pageau-St-Hilaire 2025

ISBNs: 9781009582520 (HB), 9781009582490 (PB), 9781009582513 (OC)
ISSNs: 2976-5668 (online), 2976-565X (print)

Contents

1 Introduction   1

2 Strauss's Zetetic Platonism   17

3 Gadamer's Dialogical Platonism   28

4 Patočka's Negative Platonism   43

5 Conclusion: Heidegger and the Plato Who Could Have Been   59

    List of Abbreviations   65

    Bibliography   67

1 Introduction

Heidegger's lifelong question, the question he never abandoned although he posed it in significantly different ways and terms throughout his career, is the question concerning the meaning of being (*die Frage nach dem Sinn des Seins*, SZ, 1). In the introduction to *Being and Time* (1927), Heidegger says that this question, which has now become trivialized in contemporary thinking, "is one which provided a stimulus for the researches of Plato and Aristotle" (SZ, 2). Part of the reason for this trivialization is that the meaning of Being has become allegedly so obvious and clear that we cannot see or feel the force of the question anymore. But this, he says, was not so for ancient thinkers: "that which the ancient philosophers found continually disturbing (*in die Unruhe trieb*) as something obscure and hidden (*Verborgenes*) has taken on a clarity and self-evidence such that if anyone continues to ask about it he is charged with an error of method." Heidegger elaborated his own method(s) to reawaken us to the *Seinsfrage*, and given what he says about ancient philosophy's thoughtful *perplexity* in the face of this question, it is not surprising that so much of his research both up to and after *Being and Time* was dedicated to Greek philosophy. What will be of interest to us here is, more specifically, the role of Plato and Platonism in Heidegger's sinuous path and varied attempts to revive this question with all the intensity it deserves. For as we shall see, Plato and Platonism play no small role along Heidegger's way.

In the *Contributions to Philosophy* (1936–38), Heidegger takes as a crucial task the "overcoming of Platonism." He here ties the overcoming of Platonism to the task of *Destruktion* as set out in *Being and Time*, provided that it is construed properly, namely not as a destruction (*Zerstörung*) of the tradition but as its purification (*Reinigung*) (GA 65, 221). By "purification," Heidegger here means an exposure or revealing (*Freilegen*) of fundamental metaphysical positions. This laying open must start with Plato insofar as Platonism is paradigmatic of such positions. As Heidegger will state plainly in *The End of Philosophy and the Task of Thinking* (1964), "metaphysics is Platonism" (GA 14, 71; cf. e.g. GA 6.2, 246).

Given this state of affairs, it is natural that Heidegger would try to articulate a substantial interpretation of Plato. Although he published only one essay entirely devoted to Plato during his lifetime – *Platos Lehre von der Wahrheit* (1940) – he worked out several interpretations of Plato's dialogues in various lecture courses and seminars that are now all published entirely on in part in the *Gesamtausgabe*. Between 1924 and 1942, Heidegger interpreted the *Sophist* (1924–25; in GA 19), the *Theaetetus* (1926; in GA 22), the *Parmenides* (1930–31; in GA 80), the allegory of the cave in *Republic* VII and the *Theaetetus* (1931–32 and 1933–34; in GA 34 and GA 36/37), the *Phaedrus* (1932; in GA

80), the critique of mimetic poetry in *Republic* X and the question of beauty and truth in the *Phaedrus* (1936–39; in GA 6.1), and the myth of Er in *Republic* X (1942; in GA 54). Beyond these lectures and seminars, one of course finds a plethora of fragmentary interpretations of, passing remarks on, and references to Plato throughout Heidegger's writings. Heidegger's *Auseinandersetzung* with Plato indeed plays no small role along his own *Wege*.

One characteristic trait that marks all of Heidegger's different interpretations of Plato – as well as of most philosophers of the "Western" canon – throughout the years is that they all are extraordinarily provocative. This provocative character is intimately tied to the path of *Destruktion*, an approach to the texts of the tradition that breaks off with all interpretive orthodoxies in order to let the very matter (*Sache*) that these texts are about come to light and speak anew. When Heidegger proceeded along the path of *Destruktion* in the 1920s and 1930s, his teaching thus had a decisive impact on many students, amongst whom some would later become the most prominent post-Heideggerian thinkers of the twentieth century: Günther Anders, Hannah Arendt, Hans-Georg Gadamer, Hans Jonas, Emmanuel Lévinas, Karl Löwith, Herbert Marcuse, Jan Patočka, Leo Strauss, etcetera. "Post-Heideggerian" here is no mere chronological description, but rather indicates that for them the task of philosophy is shaped by both a decisive Heideggerian inspiration and a critical intent toward that inspiration. In finding their way in this double movement from and beyond Heidegger, some of these thinkers sought to recover Aristotelian and Platonic ways of thinking in order to respond to Heidegger and to his interpretations of Greek philosophy.

Our task here is not to elucidate Heidegger's reading of Plato as a whole, but to show how three among these prominent post-Heideggerian thinkers – Leo Strauss (1899–1973), Hans-Georg Gadamer (1900–2002), and Jan Patočka (1907–77) – have criticized Heidegger and his interpretation of Plato from a Platonic standpoint, and to assess the trenchancy of their Platonic critiques. For further developed inquiries into the Platonic critiques of Heidegger offered by Leo Strauss, Hans-Georg Gadamer, as well as Gerhard Krüger, see my Heidegger and *German Platonnism: The Shadows of Marburg*, forthcoming with Cambridge University Press. However, in order to properly address Strauss, Gadamer, and Patočka as Platonic critics of Heidegger, a preparatory exposition of Heidegger's encounter with Plato is necessary.

1.1 The *Destruktion* of Greek Ontology

In *Being and Time*, Heidegger claims that a *Destruktion* of the philosophical tradition is needed for the question of Being to be genuinely recovered. The reason for this is that such tradition has become so powerful that we accept it unwittingly as self-evident and can no longer see just how much it is at work and actually influences us:

> The tradition that thus comes to domination makes proximally and for the most part what it "transmits" so little accessible that it instead conceals it. It delivers over what has come down to us to self-evidence and blocks our access to the originary "sources" out of which the categories and concepts handed down to us were in a genuine way created. (SZ, 21; my trans.)

Heidegger is quite clear that the main field of *Destruktion* must be "Greek ontology and its history," for Greek ontology has shaped our present situation by making its way through various "filiations and distorsions (*Verbiegungen*)" (SZ, 21–22). *Destruktion* is supposed to perform a dissolvement (*Ablösung*) of these concealments (*Verdeckungen*) and thus reveal and recover (*gewinnen*) in ancient ontology the original experiences wherein the first determinations of Being occurred (SZ, 22). Heidegger insists that the aim of this method is "positive" and appropriative rather than destructive in the ordinary sense: it does not seek to bury the past into nothingness (*Nichtigkeit*) (SZ, 23, cf. GA 19, 414).

Despite these promises of a positive appropriation of the original experiences at the source of the Greek interpretations of Being, Heidegger's approach to Plato and Aristotle often emphasizes the limits of their ontological thinking more than what would be worth appropriating therein. To be sure, Heidegger appropriates some key notions of Aristotle's *Rhetoric* and *Nicomachean Ethics*, and the project of fundamental ontology has often been read as developing out of such appropriations.[1] It is also significant that the epigraph to *Being and Time* is a quote from Plato's *Sophist* (244a6–8) expressing the perplexity concerning the meaning of being (ὄν), and that the work begins with an anamnesis of the "the battle of giants about being (γιγαντομαχία περὶ τῆς οὐσίας, 246a4)" (SZ, 1–2). Beyond this interrogative affinity, however, the appropriative dimension of the *Destruktion* of Aristotelian and Platonic ontology appears less clearly. Given the unfinished character of *Being and Time*, we do not have the interpretation of Aristotle that Heidegger promised there, but even the projected title of that section signals the *limits* of ancient ontology (SZ, 40). It is in fact quite clear that Heidegger had already anticipated that what the *Destruktion* of Greek ontology would reveal would amount to limitations more than actual resources:

> in our process of destruction (*Destruktion*) we find ourselves faced with the task of interpreting the soil (*Boden*) of ancient ontology in the light of the problematic of temporality (*Temporalität*). When this is done, it will be manifest that the ancient interpretation of the Being of beings is oriented

---

[1] See especially the seminal contributions of Taminiaux (1991) and Volpi (1995).

towards the "world" or "nature" in the widest sense, and that it is indeed in the terms of "time" that its understanding of Being is obtained. The outward evidence for this ... is the determination of the meaning of Being (*Sinn von Sein*) as παρουσία or οὐσία, which signifies, in ontologico-temporal terms, "presence" (*was ontologisch-temporal "Anwesenheit" bedeutet*). Entities are grasped in their Being as "presence" (*Anwesenheit*); this means that they are understood with regard to a definite mode of time – the *"Present (Gegenwart)."* (SZ, 25; trans. modif.)

In light of Heidegger's fundamental ontology, this alleged interpretation of the meaning of Being in terms of presence can only appear to him as narrow, for it precludes in principle an appreciation of the whole temporality of Dasein – one in which the three ecstases of past, present, and future are thought in their unity – which would in turn provide access to the temporality of Being itself.

Although Plato is scarcely named in *Being and Time*, the single passing and brief interpretation of a Platonic text it contains is consistent with the programmatic claim that the *Destruktion* of Greek ontology would reveal what Jacques Derrida aptly called a "metaphysics of presence." In §81, Heidegger interprets Plato as epitomizing the ordinary understanding of time as a sequence of "nows," themselves conceived as something present-at-hand (*Vorhandenes*). In allegedly reducing time to the "now," Plato reduces it to constant presence (*ständige Anwesenheit*), and this is why, we are told, the *Timaeus* interprets time by reference to eternity in calling it "the image of eternity." In the three lines quoted (*Tim.* 37d5–7), what the demiurge makes and calls "time" is actually "some moving image of eternity (εἰκὼ κινητόν τινα αἰῶνος, d5)," but Heidegger seems to have little interest in the idea that time would be an image or that it would be *moving*. I believe this brief interpretation offers us a window into the workshop of *Destruktion*. Recall that *Destruktion* is meant to bring to light the originary experiences out of which philosophical concepts arise. The difficulty is that concepts usually conceal their experiential origins, such that a dismantling interpretation must precisely go beneath the strict letter of the conceptual expression. Plato's text cited by Heidegger here does not say anything about either presence or the "now" – although Plato has words for both of these – παρουσία and νῦν – but it does mention eternity and the eternal. The kind of questions that *Destruktion* must raise is therefore: What is meant by "eternity"? What presupposition would lead one to define time in relation to "eternity"? It is in answering such questions that a "destructive" reading can claim that behind this reference to eternity lies the assumption that time is at bottom a succession of present "nows" and therefore "constant presence." But answering such questions is a daring endeavor, and in trying to bring out *das*

Ungesagte, it must in a sense always do some violence to the text. While Heidegger himself acknowledged this violence (see e.g. GA 3, 202), it should not be understood as contradicting what he elsewhere calls a "reverence toward the past" (GA 19, 414). Provided that such reverence is directed toward the very matter (*Sache*) at stake in the inquiry into the past and not the integrity of the text, it may be compatible with exegetical violence.

Heidegger's interpretations of Plato are never exempt from such violence, but it would be a great mistake to simply dismiss them on this ground. Any proper response to Heidegger's readings must instead examine whether that violence truly fulfills its promise of revealing what implicitly animates the explicit, and whether alternative interpretations of such implicit assumptions may be tenable.

1.2 Platonism and Metaphysics

In what sense does Heidegger identify Platonism with metaphysics? Although what follows should provide a clearer picture of what this identification means, we must first attempt a preliminary and general clarification concerning the notion of metaphysics. For, as Wrathall explained, the word "metaphysics" has different meanings throughout Heidegger's work. In one of these senses, metaphysics designates "one specific way of experiencing entities in the course of human history": metaphysics in this sense constitutes an *epoch* of the history of Being.[2] With respect to this meaning, Platonism occupies a pivotal role, for it is indeed the instigator of this metaphysical epoch, the arc of which reaches, Heidegger claims, from Plato to Nietzsche. In another sense, metaphysics refers to discrete metaphysical positions defended by various thinkers *within* the metaphysical stage of the history of Being. What interests Heidegger the most in these different metaphysical "theories" is not so much the explicit metaphysical claims defended by these philosophers, but rather the underlying "background assumptions" that together sustain an implicit understanding of Being.[3] Precisely as implicit "background views," metaphysics in this sense is often if not always somewhat unthought (*ungedacht*) and therefore unsaid (*ungesagt*). This is why Heidegger thinks the task of the interpreter of such metaphysical views must always try to go through the text and yet beyond the text. As he puts it in *Kant and the Problem of Metaphysics*, the reader must move through what is said (*durch das Gesagte*) toward what remains unsaid (*das Ungesagte*) (GA 3, 201). It also explains why Heidegger can claim that someone who explicitly opposes the metaphysical tradition may nonetheless operate according to metaphysical assumptions: Nietzsche thus appears no less metaphysical a thinker

---

[2] Wrathall (2021, 486).   [3] See Wrathall (2021, e.g. 488).

than Plato. In view of metaphysics in this latter sense, Plato's role is also central, for uncovering the implicit understanding of Being out of which his apparent or explicit metaphysical claims (albeit unwittingly) unfold amounts to nothing else than revealing the first articulation of the background theses concerning the meaning of Being and truth that would govern the entirety of metaphysics in the former sense – that is, the metaphysical epoch of human history. Accordingly, there is a sense in which, when Heidegger proclaims the identity of metaphysics and Platonism, the two senses of metaphysics I just described coincide. The fate of metaphysics and the fate of Platonism are thus, per Heidegger, indistinguishable. Whether Heidegger's attempt to overcome that metaphysics results in some genuinely postmetaphysical thinking or something like a renewal of metaphysics in a completely different sense[4] may be left open here, as long as this much is clear: neither does Heidegger think he is doing metaphysics in the senses just discussed, nor does he think it is possible to genuinely recover Plato or Platonism for the new kind of thinking he calls for.[5] In this decisive respect Strauss, Gadamer, and Patočka disagree with Heidegger.

Before turning to Heidegger's interpretation of such background metaphysics in Plato, a further clarificatory remark may be apropos. One wonders if there is a difference, on Heidegger's view, between Plato and Platonism. Answering this question requires a distinction. Certainly, Heidegger thinks there is a difference between Plato's thinking and the Platonism(s) that unfolded thereafter, and he is quite explicit that interpreting Plato through the lens of these Platonic traditions is seriously misleading: "to want to interpret Plato with the help of any kind of Platonism is a genuine spoilage (*eigentliche Verderb*). For this procedure is just like that which attempts to 'explain' the fresh leaf in the tree based on the fallen foliage on the ground" (GA 54, 143; my trans.). In fact, would he think otherwise, the whole task of *Destruktion* would make no sense. But Platonism can be understood in another sense, the sense precisely sought for by *Destruktion*: the underlying, background theses that may unwittingly inform Plato's actual thinking. That kind of Platonism is not post-Platonic; it is not the fallen leaves next to the tree of Plato's philosophy, but rather something like the roots of the tree. That subterranean, subtly yet decisively operative Platonism is

---

[4] As Gadamer sometimes suggests (e.g. GW 10, 105). In spite of Heidegger's critique, metaphysics has recently experienced a strong resurgence in various traditions. One can think of analytic, neo-Aristotelian, or neo-Thomist metaphysics. This could mean that Heidegger's critique did not have a very enduring effect. But it could also simply be an indication that contemporary philosophy moves in increasingly specialized and relatively "closed" fields wherein philosophers think they are "exempt" from addressing Heidegger's critique of metaphysics: *some* contemporary philosophers address that critique (one can think of Brague and Gonzalez with respect to Plato and Aristotle, or of Rioux with respect to St. Thomas Aquinas), but *very few* do.

[5] See Gadamer's explicit remark about this (EE, 170).

what Heidegger is trying to uproot by figuring out what remained unsaid and unthought in Plato's works. And that very Platonism, Heidegger thinks, is metaphysics in the senses just discussed.

The portrait of Plato Heidegger developed between 1924 and 1942 is certainly not monolithic and changeless. There are, however, running threads in his interpretations, theses that, once elaborated, continuously reemerge and come to dominate his otherwise often sensitive and highly perceptive readings. The first of these theses is that Plato understands Being as presence. The second is that Plato is responsible for the occlusion of the original understanding of truth as unconcealedness (*Unverborgenheit*, ἀλήθεια) and its transformation into correctness (*Richtigkeit*, ὀρθότης), which paves the way to the correspondence theory of truth that prevails to this day. Taken together, these two alleged Platonic mistakes amount to a metaphysics that reduces Being to what can susceptibly fall under human (cognitive) mastery. In this very sense, Heidegger claims that Platonism as metaphysics prefigures Nietzsche's metaphysics of the will-to-power (e.g. GA 6.2, 198–202, 210–15, 245–46), and that they both culminate in nihilism (see GA 65, 219). Thusly seen, Platonic philosophy is the inception of the oblivion of Being. How does that narrative unfold?

1.2.1 Plato's Metaphysics of Presence

The first thesis already emerges in the 1924–25 *Sophist* lectures. There, Heidegger indeed translates quite systematically οὐσία as presence (*Anwesenheit*). The justification for this choice is apparently that "the meaning of Being (*der Sinn von Sein*) that implicitly (*unausdrücklich*) guides this [i.e. Greek] ontology is that Being = presence (*Sein* = *Anwesenheit*)" (GA 19, 466). This in turn Heidegger connects to the idea that the ordinary meaning of οὐσία in Greek is one's domain (*Besitz*), household (*Hausstand*), or property (*Anwesen*) (467). But how does one see this interpretation at play in Plato's *Sophist* if it is only implicit and not expressed as such? Heidegger turns our attention to the Eleatic Stranger's account of the meaning of producing (ποιεῖν) as a "leading into Being (ἄγειν εἰς οὐσίαν, cf. *Soph.* 219b4)" (269). From this he infers not just that οὐσία *can* be produced, but that Being *in general* means "to be produced (*Hergestelltsein*)" (270). There is a clear hermeneutic violence here: what applies to production is generalized to Being in general. Of course, such generalization would be less problematic if Heidegger was right to assume that production *is* the ontological paradigm of Greek philosophy. But rightly or not, that is indeed Heidegger's view. The thesis that Plato understands Being as presence thus seems predicated on the view that Being for him (as for "the

Greeks" in general) means producedness, for producedness entails presence: "therefore, Being signifies, in a wholly determinate sense, *the presence of definite things in the circuit of everyday use (Gebrauch) and everyday sight (Sehen)*" (269).

Heidegger holds on to this thesis with a remarkable insistence, even when in his reading of the *Sophist* he encounters insights that seem to run against the interpretation of Being as presence. The most notable case of that insistence is his interpretation of the Stranger's determination of Being as power or potentiality (δύναμις). This potentiality is more specifically a "potentiality to affect and to be affected (δύναμις εἴτ' εἰς τὸ ποιεῖν εἴτ' εἰς τὸ παθεῖν, 247d8–e;1; cf. 248c4–5: ἡ τοῦ πάσχειν ἢ δρᾶν δύναμις)." How is such a dynamic conception of Being compatible with constant presence? Heidegger in fact acknowledges there that Being thus understood means "possibility (*Möglichkeit*)" (GA 19, 475). This understanding of Being as the power to affect and be affected proves essential in the dialogue's attempt to account for the "community of the kinds (κοινωνία τῶν γενῶν)," namely Being's ability to mix with the other great kinds – motion, rest, sameness and otherness. When the δύναμις of Being is further determined as the capacity to "share with," "mix with," or "be in community with" (κοινωνεῖν), Heidegger seems to admit that the "sense of Being (*Sinn von Sein*)" that is at stake is the possibility "to be with one another (*Miteinandersein*)" and "to be related to one another (*Aufeinanderbezogensein*)" (478–79). It is once more hardly possible to harmonize this understanding of Being with presence, and if we allow ourselves to read this retrospectively in light of *Being and Time*, one would need to admit that *Miteinandersein* as a mode of Being is absolutely antithetic to presence-at-hand (*Vorhandenheit*). Despite this opposition, Heidegger reintroduces presence without any explicit justification: "*Being means nothing other than: being-able-to-be-with-one-another (Miteinandersein-Können)*, or formulated differently, in relation to Being as δύναμις, *being-capable toward presence alongside something (Imstande-sein zur Anwesenheit bei etwas)*" (480). He then reformulates "differently" *Miteinandersein* as "copresence (*Mitanwesenheit*)." Of course, these represent no mere "different" formulations of the same idea but rather two completely distinct views. For indeed *Anwesenheit* captures neither the dynamic nor the relational dimensions of the understanding of Being that Heidegger encounters in these passages.[6] As Heidegger gives us no explicit reason for such radical "reformulations," we are left to think that the implicit motivation behind these reinterpretations is his unshakable conviction that Plato understands Being fundamentally as presence. But again, this conviction is the result of another conviction, namely that Being for the Greeks (Plato included) means "to be

---

[6] This point has been aptly discussed by both Figal (2000, 107–8) and Gonzalez (2009, 87–93).

produced." This raises a question: can the identification of Platonic ontology with a metaphysics of presence be maintained if the thesis according to which *Sein = Hergestelltsein* is erroneous?

In 1931–32 (and 1933–34), Heidegger articulates an interpretation of Plato's putative understanding of Being as presence that does not rely entirely on the paradigm of production. Recall that the consequence of producedness was understood as a presence for both use (*Gebrauch*) and seeing (*Sehen*). If presence for sight can be divorced from producedness in Plato, then there could be a metaphysics of presence without the productionist paradigm. This is just what Heidegger seems to be working out in his interpretation of Platonic Forms. The first step in this interpretation is the claim that Forms are Plato's equivalent for the Being of beings (*das Sein des Seiendes*) (GA 34, 51–52; cf. GA 36/37, 152, 161). Second, Heidegger recalls that the words Plato uses for Forms – εἶδος and ἰδέα – are both related to seeing (ἰδεῖν) "Ἰδέα is that which gives itself and is there for and in ἰδεῖν, in seeing, to which there corresponds what is seen, what is sighted (*das Gesehene, Gesichtete*)" (GA 34, 48; modif. trans.) Thus the Form of something is its "aspect" or "look" (*Anblick*). Such a "look," however, is not accessible to a mere sense-perceptual seeing: it involves understanding of "what *is* there (was da *ist*)" (GA 34, 50).

A Form is therefore the look through which some entity "offers and showcases itself (*sich an- und darbietet*)" as what it is (GA 34, 51). Apparently extrapolating on the meaning of these verbs (*anbieten* and *darbieten*), Heidegger arrives at the third and final step of his interpretation of ἰδέα: "It is through these looks (Anblicke) that individual things *present* themselves [sich *präsentiert*] as this and that, is present and *present* (präsent und *anwesend* ist)" (51; modif. trans.). In the 1933–34 lectures, Heidegger plays on this same verb (*darbieten*) to say that a Form presents (*darstellt*) the thing's self-presence (*Selbstgegenwart*; GA 36/37, 152). Thus, the meaning of Being implied in Platonic Forms is *presence for sight*.

We may of course wonder whether the self-presentation of something in and through its Form is the same as presence. Heidegger here indeed moves quite freely between the movement of presenc*ing* (*präsentieren, anwesen*) and the state of something being present – that is, its presence (*Präsenz, Gegenwart, Anewsenheit*). In both lecture courses on the allegory of the cave, the conflation of these two potentially different phenomena appears to be justified by recalling that "presence for the Greeks means Being" (GA 34, 51; cf. GA 36/37, 152). Be that as it may, as long as Forms are not understood as produced, Heidegger's reading identifies a Platonic metaphysics of presence without recurring to the paradigm of production. In the *Nietzsche* lectures, however, Forms are interpreted as demiurgically produced, and so the two theses about the meaning of

Being for Plato, after having been for some time disjoined, seem to come back together: *Sein = Hergestelltsein = Anwesenheit*.[7]

This alleged metaphysics of presence poses two problems for Heidegger. First, there is the problem of time: as we have seen from the passage of *Being and Time* quoted earlier (SZ, 25), interpreting Being as presence unduly gives precedence to the present over and against both past and future. This primacy of presence obstructs any attempt to genuinely understand Being in terms of its temporality because it gives the highly misleading impression that it does not interpret Being temporally while it in fact does. Heidegger is quite explicit about this point at the end of *Introduction to Metaphysics*:

> But why time, precisely? Because in the inception of Western philosophy, the *perspective that guides* the opening up of Being is time, but *in such a way* that this perspective *as such* still remained and had to remain concealed (*verborgen*). If what finally becomes the fundamental concept of Being is οὐσία, and this means constant presence (*ständige Anwesenheit*), then what lies unexposed (*unenthüllt*) as the ground of the essence of stability (*Beständigkeit*) and the essence of presence (*Wesen der Anwesenheit*), other than time? (EM, 157/GA 40, 215)

Second, the understanding of Being as presence grants priority to presence over and against absence, and thereby gives the illusion that there can be complete, full, or constant presence without absence. What this picture suggests is that Being steadily reveals itself without withdrawing or concealing itself. Heidegger insists that we should instead think of presence and absence as thoroughly intertwined, just like we should think of unconcealment and concealment in their mutual belonging. The second issue with Plato's metaphysics of presence thus points to the question of truth.

1.2.2 Plato's Transformation of the Essence of Truth

According to Heidegger, two radically different conceptions of truth cohabit in Plato's thought. On the one hand, Plato thinks of truth as ἀ-λήθεια, namely the privation of λήθη, of concealment. Thus understood, truth is the un-concealedness (*Un-verborgenheit*) of beings, and the privative aspect of the word points to the idea that beings are ordinarily concealed and thus have to be teared out of their concealedness to come into their open manifestness. On the other hand, Plato also conceives of truth as "correctness" (ὀρθότης, *Richtigkeit*). This second conception, Heidegger thinks, is the forerunner of the notion of truth as the correctness of assertions – that is, the view that truth designates the agreement or correspondence

---

[7] GA 6.1, 186. This interpretation of Forms was already advanced in 1927 (GA 24, 405) but seems to have been abandoned until the *Nietzsche* lectures. On this, see also Dostal (1985, 87 and 98).

between a subject's judgment and its object. In criticizing that view, Heidegger does not intend to get rid of it. The problem is not that truth is *not* correctness, but that such correctness always presupposes a prior disclosure of the phenomenon such that our judgments or assertions can in turn correspond to it (cf. GA 34, 3). However, proponents of the correspondence theory of truth usually fail to acknowledge the necessity of such prior disclosure. When the ontological priority of unconcealedness over correctness is misconstrued or overlooked, the forgetfulness of truth begins. Heidegger thinks that Plato both saw the priority relation properly *and* misconstrued it. Because he sees in Plato's thinking both moments, he claims that, in Plato, the essence of truth is transformed.

Heidegger's privileged textual locus for the interpretation of Plato's understanding of truth is the allegory of the cave in book 7 of the *Republic*. At the end of book 6, the analogy of the sun had depicted truth as light (*Resp.* 507e4–509a5), and light is indeed the guiding image for thinking about truth inside and outside the cave. Heidegger emphasizes that even the shadows that the prisoners see before they are freed are for them "the true (τὸ ἀληθές)." This indicates, he claims, that truth has nothing to do with the correctness or correspondence of judgments and is rather the unconcealedness of things (GA 34, 25–30). The shadows are "the true" insofar as they are what is manifest to the prisoners. The notion of correctness emerges in Plato's allegory when the prisoners are unshackled and forced to look at the puppets that produce the shadows they were previously seeing. They are then told that they now see more correctly (ὀρθότερον βλέποι) since they are turned toward things that *are more* (μᾶλλον ὄντα, "mehr seiend, *seiender*") (515d3–4; GA 34, 32–34; GA 36/37, 137–38). Heidegger's observation about this passage is acute and very important. The correctness of the prisoners' sight is wholly dependent on them seeing beings that are more and thus (should) appear more vividly, as more unconcealed: "*Truth as correctness is impossible without truth as unconcealment*. ... The concept of correctness already brings unconcealment with it" (GA 36/37, 139; cf. GA 34, 34). In these initial stages, then, Plato seems to understand the priority relation of ἀλήθεια and ὀρθότης properly.

It is indeed not before we reach Heidegger's interpretation of the Idea of the Good that we begin to see Plato's alleged transformation of the essence of truth. In the sun analogy (507a–509b), Socrates compares the Good to the sun, and truth to light. Just like light operates as the yoke (ζυγόν) that unites seeing and the seen (ὁρᾶν and ὁρώμενα), truth is the yoke that ties together intelligence and the intelligible (νοεῖν and νοούμενα). But since the Good is responsible (αἴτιος) for truth like the sun is responsible for light (508b9), Heidegger insists that truth is itself under the yoke of the Idea of the Good (GA 36/37, 205). The issue here is not so much that truth is yoked by the Good, but that it now stands under the *Idea* of the Good. In the 1931–32 and 1933–34 interpretations of the allegory of the cave, Heidegger does not yet explain how this subordination of truth as ἀλήθεια to the Idea of the Good brings with it the overtaking of correctness as the predominant sense of truth. That story is told in Heidegger's 1940 reinterpretation of the allegory of the cave, "Platos Lehre von der Wahrheit." However, two crucial premises of his argument are already laid out in 1931–32: (1) as we have seen, Heidegger interprets the Platonic ἰδέα in terms of its seeing (ἰδεῖν); (2) he interprets the Idea of the Good not as radically different from other Forms but as the "highest Idea," namely the Idea that performs in the most originary and genuine way (*am ursprünglichsten und eigentlichsten*) the *same* function or "job" (*Amt*) as that of any Idea, namely to let see the Being of beings (GA 34, 99). What the 1940 interpretation adds to these premises is that with the seeing of the Ideas comes the requisite of a *correct* seeing:

> if our comportment with beings is always and everywhere a matter of the ἰδεῖν of the ἰδέα, the seeing of the 'visible form' (*das Erblicken des 'Aussehens'*), then all our efforts must be concentrated above all on making such seeing possible. And that requires the correct vision (*das rechte Blicken*). (GA 9, 230)

Subordinating truth as unconcealedness to Forms thus means subordinating it to the correctness of our seeing (and *in extenso* of proposition [*Aussagen*]). With this new configuration, truth is no longer "a fundamental trait of beings themselves (*Grundzug des Seienden selbst*)" but becomes a function of the human subject (GA 9, 231, cf. 238). This transformation marks the "beginning of metaphysics" in Plato's thinking (236) – that is, the beginning of a tradition that culminates in Nietzsche's reversed Platonism and nihilism (233, 237, cf. GA 65, 219).

In his 1942–43 course on Parmenides, Heidegger returns to Plato and proposes a seeming revision of his narrative concerning truth. There, his attention to the myth of Er in book 10 of the *Republic* leads him to acknowledge that Plato has seen that unconcealedness (ἀλήθεια) and concealedness (λήθη) belong together (GA 54, 183–85). In light of his new discovery, Heidegger faults the Roman latinization of the Greek experience of truth for occluding the essence of truth as unconcealedness. *Veritas* no longer evokes the play of concealment and unconcealment; *falsum* as a translation of ψεῦδος makes us lose sight of the fact that ψεῦδος is not just a falsification but a concealing that at once reveals (as in the meaning of the word "pseudonym") (64–65, cf. 43–44 and GA 36/37, 227); *rectitudo* as a translation of ὁμοίωσις reduces once and for all truth to the correctness of a proposition (73). It would be hasty, however, to conclude from this that Heidegger abandoned his thesis concerning Plato's inceptive metaphysics. While Plato *did* think through the mutual belonging of ἀλήθεια and λήθη, he is also guilty of a subjectivizing interpretation of λήθη as a human forgetting instead of the concealment inherent to Being itself:

> Plato inaugurates, along with the transformation of the essence of ἀλήθεια into ὁμοίοσις, a transformation of λήθη and of the ἀνάμνησις opposing it. The event of the withdrawing concealment (*Das Ereignis der entziehenden Verbergung*) transforms itself into the human comportment of forgetting. Similarly, what is opposed to λήθη becomes a re-retrieving through the human being (*Wiederzurück-holen durch den Menschen*). (185; trans. modif.)

Despite the epochal role of the Roman appropriation of Greek insights into the Latin world and language in Heidegger's *Seinsgeschichte*, Plato remains responsible for occluding the originary sense of truth and setting in motion the metaphysical tradition that Heidegger will attempt to overcome through most of his work.

1.3 A Destruktion of the Destruktion? Strauss, Gadamer, Patočka

The *Destruktion* of Plato thus leads Heidegger to construe an onto-historical narrative wherein Socrates' pupil is the instigator of a tradition that has lost the power of even posing genuinely the question of Being. Despite this or more likely because of this, many among Heidegger's students were more impressed with the promise of Heidegger's *Destruktion* of Greek philosophy than with the conclusions that he drew from it. Could new reactivations of Platonic philosophy be attempted? Could it possible to leap back to Plato through and yet beyond Heidegger's *Destruktion*? Could one articulate a *Destruktion* of his *Destruktion*? Such is, as I shall argue here, the Platonic path of Leo Strauss, Hans-Georg Gadamer, and Jan Patočka.

Strauss encountered Heidegger for the first time in Freiburg in 1922. Hearing him lecture on Aristotle was a genuine turning point in his own philosophical awakening:

> I said to [Rosenzweig] that, in comparison with Heidegger, Weber appeared to me as an "orphan child" in regard to precision and probing and competence. I had never seen before such seriousness, profundity, and concentration in the interpretation of philosophic texts. I had heard Heidegger's interpretation of certain sections in Aristotle, and some time later I heard Werner Jaeger in Berlin interpret the same texts. Charity compels me to limit my comparison to the remark that there was no comparison. . . . We saw with our own eyes that there had been no such phenomenon in the world since Hegel. (RCPR, 28)

Strauss credited phenomenological *Destruktion* for opening a new access to the Greeks, an access unfiltered by either modern presuppositions or medieval scholasticism. Once freed up, this possibility of returning to Greek philosophy needed not turn into a critique like it did for Heidegger. Thus Heidegger opened up new possibilities "without intending it":

> Above all, his intention was to uproot Aristotle: he thus was compelled to disinter the roots, to bring them to light, to look at them with wonder. Klein was the first to understand the possibility which Heidegger had opened without intending it: the possibility of a genuine return to classical philosophy, to the philosophy of Aristotle and of Plato, a return with open eyes and in full clarity about the infinite difficulties which it entails. (JPCM, 450)

As early as 1934, Strauss would speak in his private correspondence of his own intellectual trajectory as a "way beyond Heidegger (*Richtung über Heidegger hinaus*)."[8]

Gadamer encountered Heidegger in 1923 in Freiburg, after having read the so-called *Natorp-Bericht*, in which Heidegger presented to Natorp the program of his research on Aristotle. Gadamer recalled several times how great the influence of this text on his first philosophical impulse was (GW 10, 33, cf. HTJ, 229).[9] He thus wrote his habilitation under Heidegger's supervision. Its result was his first work on Plato, *Platos dialektische Ethik: Phänomenologische Interpretationen zum Philebos* (1931), a text that both acknowledges his debt to Heidegger and signals his attempt to "extend" his master's phenomenological method and to "make it fruitful by practicing it in a new way" (PDE, xxvi). Retrospectively, Gadamer said that Heidegger's *Destruktion* has left an important heritage. Heidegger

> simply knew how to liberate the plurivocity of words and the inner gravitational force of the living use of words with its conceptual implications, while also sharpening our sense for them. This was the positive sense of the word "deconstruction" (*Destruktion*), in which there are no echoes of "destruction" (*Zerstörung*). (GW 10, 45; HG, 37)

Despite this positive sense of *Destruktion*, and despite the fact that it is not meant to *destroy* the texts of the past, Gadamer nonetheless saw in it an interpretive violence quite antithetical to the hermeneutic principles that Gadamer would develop: "When he had to interpret 'texts,' then I often had difficulties with it, because he violently bent the texts to fit his own intentions"

---

[8] GS 3, 494. For biographical-philological evidences that Strauss understands himself as following the method of *Destruktion*, see Ciccarelli (2018, 20–21).

[9] See Taminiaux (2004).

(GW 10, 45; HG, 37).[10] Among Gadamer's disagreements with Heidegger's *Destruktion* of the Greeks, the most serious one concerns the Heideggerian interpretation of Plato: "Only the thought-event of the Platonic dialogues – the first philosophical text that we still have – remained inaccessible to this impatient questioner in spite of all of the momentum behind his appropriations" (GW 3, 289; HW, 144). Heidegger's readings of Plato therefore represent, as Gadamer himself said, a "continuous challenge" for him.[11]

Patočka studied with both Husserl and Heidegger in Freiburg in the early 1930s and elaborated his own phenomenological thinking. Two closely intertwined features of Patočka's phenomenology are particularly striking. First, it is highly sensitive to Heidegger's critique of metaphysics and endorses much of it. Second, its center of gravity is the concept of "care for the soul" (*péče o duši*), a notion he appropriates from the Platonic Socrates' injunction (ἐπιμελεῖσθαι τῆς ψυχῆς, *Apol.* 30b1–2, cf. *Alc. I* 132c1). It is impossible to understand Patočka's project without grasping how he attempts to harmonize these two apparently contradictory characteristics. In a nutshell, Patočka thinks we can and should make a distinction within Platonic philosophy itself. On the one hand, there is the "negative" or Socratic moment of Platonism. On the other hand, there is the dogmatic moment of Platonism, the moment in which the Socratic interrogation is answered and wholly replaced by the answer. The essence of metaphysics consists in occluding the Socratic question by an answer (NP, 181). The apparent paradox of Patočka's negative Platonism is that it does not relinquish the conceptual apparatus that one usually associates with the "doctrinal" content of Platonism, most notably the notions of the soul, of Forms, and of their "separation." Patočka rather thinks it is possible to interpret such notions both nonmetaphysically and metaphysically. And this is why he thinks that a post-Heideggerian phenomenology can be Platonic.

In emphasizing the Socratic and interrogative dimensions of Plato's thinking, Patočka is very close to Strauss and Gadamer, who both place Socratic questioning and *docta ignorantia* at the center of Platonic philosophy.[12] Like Patočka, Strauss and Gadamer too interpret Plato's alleged "metaphysics" through this Socratic matrix. Their interpretations allow a new picture of Plato to emerge, one that is hardly vulnerable to Heidegger's attack against Platonism as metaphysics and metaphysics as Platonism. In a very broad sense, the Platonic critique of Heidegger developed by Strauss, Gadamer, and Patočka

---

[10] In *Heidegger's Ways*, Gadamer says that Heidegger delivered "coercive interpretations" of texts in which he "heard and rediscovered only himself" (GW 3, 288; HW, 143).

[11] See IG, 5; GW 7, 130 and Dostal (1997).

[12] Thus Renaud (1999) aptly calls Gadamer's Platonic path a "Resocratizing" (*Resokratisierung*) of Plato.

alike could be summed up as follows: by condemning Platonism as the beginning of metaphysics and leaping back to pre-Socratic poetic thinking, Heidegger is oblivious of the Socratic possibilities that stand between early Greek thinking and "Platonic" dogmatism.

Recovering the Socratic soil of Platonic philosophy allows Strauss, Gadamer, and Patočka to open up the possibility that Plato did not in fact philosophize within the productionist paradigm that Heidegger thinks underlies the "Greek conception of Being" – that is, the understanding of Being as constant presence. For all three of them, the fundamental experience in which all of Plato's philosophy is grounded is not production, but human existence understood in its ethical-political facticity. The proper starting point is not productive but active; to speak in Aristotelian terms, it is human πρᾶξις and not ποίησις. Platonic "theory," for them, is never torn apart from this practical character of human life. It is only when this principle is violated and philosophical speculation is divorced from this basic human activity that ossified doctrines can enter the scene and something like a metaphysics of presence becomes possible.

With these new interpretations of Plato come new historical-philosophical narratives that offer alternatives to Heidegger's *Seinsgeschichte*. For Heidegger, the oblivion of Being begins with the metaphysical epoch inaugurated by Plato. From Plato onward, the history of Western thinking is the history of a decline. For Strauss and Patočka, it is rather the oblivion of the Socratic-Platonic origins of Western philosophy that is responsible for the decline. Strauss indeed claims that the Western tradition has progressively forgotten the original meaning of political philosophizing, and there are indications that he identifies the beginning of this forgetting already in Aristotle's transformation of political *philosophy* into political *science*.[13] As for Patočka, a central claim of his whole philosophical work, epitomized in his late lectures entitled *Plato and Europe* (1973), is that Europe has come to an end because it has completely forgotten its vital guiding principle, namely the Socratic-Platonic "care for the soul." While Gadamer was always skeptical of narratives of grand declines such as Heidegger's,[14] he seems to see in *Aristotle* and not in Plato the beginning of Western metaphysics (e.g. GW 3, 238; HW, 81). It is also quite clear that he sees in Plato the dialogical model of hermeneutic experience that can be an antidote to the modern primacy of method in the *Geisteswissenschaften*.[15] And in the foreword to the second edition of *Truth and Method*, Gadamer says that hermeneutics opposes to the modern human will the "truth of remembrance

---

[13] See CM, 21 and Collins (2015).

[14] In their correspondence, Strauss sides, *against* Gadamer, with Heidegger on this very issue of the history of philosophy as a declining one (see esp. CWM, 8 and 11).

[15] See GW 1, 368–75.

(*Wahrheit des Errinerns*)" (GW 2, 448; TM, xxxv). This is to say that despite his reluctance to articulate an explicit revision of Heidegger's historical-philosophical narrative, there is a sense in which Gadamer's hermeneutics can be understood as an anamnesis of Plato amidst the ruins of a world dominated by "total technocracy" and its ensuing *Seinsvergessenheit* (GW 2, 447; TM, xxxiv). But here again, Plato is not responsible for the oblivion; rather the oblivion of Plato is responsible for the contemporary crisis.

* * *

In what follows, I present the great lines of the Platonic critiques of Heidegger developed by Strauss, Gadamer, and Patočka, and ask what kind of Heideggerian rejoinders they could prompt. In Section 2, I discuss Strauss' phenomenological interpretation of dialogue and dialectic in Plato, his ensuing understanding of Platonic Forms as questions, as well as his view concerning the fundamental elusiveness of Being. Section 3 turns to Gadamer's interpretation of Plato's dialectical ethics, of Forms in general, and of the Good, the Beautiful, and truth in particular. In Section 4, I examine Patočka's conception of negative Platonism, of care for the soul, and his narrative concerning the Platonic roots of Europe. In the Conclusion, I sketch how some of Heidegger's own undeveloped considerations on Plato and Socrates could have converged with the Platonic critiques of Strauss, Gadamer, and Patočka.

2 Strauss's Zetetic Platonism

Strauss thinks that Plato's decision to write in a dialogical form deserves our keenest attention. In light of the *Phaedrus*' critique of writing, Strauss thinks that we "may assume that the Platonic dialogue is a kind of writing which is free from the essential defect of writings" (CM, 52). In the Myth of Theuth in the *Phaedrus*, writing is criticized according to the standard set by living speeches: writings cannot answer back their readers, and it cannot speak differently to different people (*Phdr.*, 275e). They thus run the risk of being reduced to a set of self-standing propositions at the disposal of the reader's potentially dogmatic use. Strauss thinks Plato turned to the dialogical form precisely to avoid this. He sharply contrasts Platonic dialogues with Aristotelian treatises to highlight the hermeneutic problem of Plato's authorial anonymity: "Whereas in reading the *Politics* we hear Aristotle all the time, in reading the *Republic* we hear Plato never. In none of his dialogues does Plato ever say anything" (CM, 50).

This does not mean, of course, that we cannot understand a Platonic dialogue. Rather, in order to do so, one cannot rely on the interlocutors' speeches alone, and must scrutinize the complex interweaving of the speeches and the broader action and situational context of these dialogues. For Strauss, however, this is not a mere device employed by Plato to conceal his doctrines. The mimetic character of the dialogue is of importance here: in imitating specific, concrete, lived conversations, Plato draws our attention to dialogue not just as a form of written presentation but as a way of philosophizing. Strauss originally claims that both these dialectical conversations and their Platonic imitations are more radically phenomenological than any philosophical treatise could ever be, and he thinks this is true in two senses: it is more faithful to the phenomenon of philosophical inquiry, and it is more faithful to the phenomena under investigation in such inquiry.

2.1 Dialogue, Dialectic, and Political Phenomenology

Like the young Heidegger whom he encountered in the 1920s, Strauss thinks that ancient philosophy's way of inquiring is more attuned to the phenomena than the modern way. Whereas ancient thinkers – Strauss here thinks chiefly of Plato and Aristotle – proceed in a "movement" going "from opinion to knowledge" or "from the here and now to what is always," modern philosophers move in the opposite way, namely "from the abstract towards the concrete" (WIPP, 28). But as both Husserl and Heidegger had seen, taking as one's point of departure theoretical concepts instead of the given phenomena always runs the risk of blurring or distorting them. Strauss perfectly agrees with them on this point: the modern way of inquiring misses the concrete and is "untrue to the phenomena" (29).

Platonic dialogues, on the contrary, depict philosophy in all its concreteness, and so start with the existential situatedness of philosophical inquiry as lived out by its interlocutors (OPS, 73). This sits well with Heidegger's view that any theoretical comportment of Dasein must be understood as a projected possibility rooted in a more primordial situation, of being-in-the-world as determined by Dasein's facticity and thrownness (SZ, 56, 135). By depicting philosophy as arising from what Drew Hyland aptly called its "situational finitude,"[16] Platonic dialogues seem to anticipate the idea that proximally and for the most part, human beings do not consider things disinterestedly as objects but rather as things with which they are concerned. Strauss agrees with Heidegger that "our primary understanding of the world is not an understanding of things as objects but of what the Greeks indicated by *pragmata*" (RCPR, 29), and he thinks this is clearly shown in Plato's way of presenting philosophical activity. But he disagrees quite clearly with Heidegger on how to interpret such πράγματα. For Heidegger, the originary encounter with entities is one in which they appear as ready-to-hand (*zuhanden*), and so for him πρᾶγμα chiefly means "tool"

---

[16] See Hyland (1995).

(*Zeug*, SZ, 68). While Heidegger claims that this account of our concerned dealing with πράγματα corresponds to the Greek notion of πρᾶξις (action), Strauss implicitly responds that what Heidegger is getting at is actually closer to ποίησις (production). What we primarily care for and are concerned with is not the world of tools, but the ethical-political nexus of signification in which we inevitably orient ourselves. In this sense, it seems like Strauss is accusing Heidegger of remaining at a too abstract level when he deals with our average everydayness ontologically. A too strictly ontological inquiry can hardly see that the world of Dasein's being-in-the-world is always already the world of the political community, of the πόλις.

Accordingly, not only do Platonic dialogues point to the political facticity of their interlocutors, but the very questions they tackle are those that emerge from that inescapable political embeddedness. This is not to say that Plato's works do not inquire into more "ultimate" and ontological questions such as "what is truth?" or "what is Being?" They undoubtedly do. Strauss' point is rather that the dialogues never start with these questions. Rather, such questions unfold from examinations of issues that the interlocutors, as political beings, are intimately concerned with. For instance, the question of truth and its relation to being in the *Republic* is arrived at from the initial question "what is justice?" Similarly, the question of Being and non-Being in the *Sophist* unravels from a broader and prior interrogation concerning the difference between the philosopher, sophist, and the statesman, a question that Socrates is deeply interested in practically: he is about to defend himself in court against the accusation of being some kind of corrupting sophist. In this way, Platonic dialogues are truer to the phenomena than ontological treatises because they always start with the phenomena that stand out and appear the most to us – that is, *practical* phenomena. Strauss thus provocatively writes: "[Socrates] still remains chiefly ... concerned with the human things: with what is by nature right and noble or with the nature of justice and nobility. In its original form political philosophy broadly understood is the core of philosophy or rather 'the first philosophy'" (CM, 20).

Dialectical inquiry, as imitated by the Platonic compositions, is also faithful to this kind of political phenomenology in its methodology. By dialectic, Strauss chiefly means elenctic cross-examination. Dialectic is phenomenological insofar as, in trying to grapple with the ethical-political questions humans are concerned with in the world of the πόλις, it starts with what is first available to the inquirer: opinions (CM, 20). This, Strauss contends, is no arbitrary choice. He draws from the autobiographical passage of Plato's *Phaedo*, where Socrates tells the story of his philosophical reorientation. This reorientation was the result of his dissatisfaction with the philosophical inquiry of physicists like Anaxagoras. By inquiring directly into perceptible phenomena, Anaxagoras arrived merely at material causal explanations, namely explanations that can hardly account for human phenomena such as Socrates deciding to stay in prison and drink the hemlock instead of escaping (*Phd.* 98c–d). In light of his dissatisfaction, Socrates instead resolved to inquire indirectly into the nature of things by turning to human speeches (λόγοι, *Phd.* 99d4–100a7). About Socrates' "second navigation," Strauss writes: "Plato 'takes refuge' from things in human speech about things as the *only entrance* into the true reasons of things which is open to man" (PPH, 141). The phenomenological turn to speeches that dialectic represents is therefore no mere second-best option: "to give up the orientation by speech means giving up the only possible orientation, which is originally at the disposal of men" (PPH, 153).

From a Heideggerian standpoint, we may legitimately ask whether ordinary human speech is a suitable basis for philosophical inquiry. Is not everyday speech shallow, contradictory, and always likely to devolve into chatter and idle talk (*Gerede*)? Strauss concedes this but interestingly thinks that the instability of ordinary human speech can set the dialectician on the right path: "the fact that what men say is contradictory proves that there is truth hidden in what they say" (PPH, 143). For Strauss, such truth lies in the intentionality of the speeches themselves, as distinguished from what the speakers might think they intend: "whenever we speak of virtue ... whether we characterize temperance, courage or justice as virtue – we, in all these cases, use the same word virtue, we always *mean* the same thing" (141–42; my emphasis).[17] Of course, citizens disagree about what virtue is, and that is because they disagree about what the good is, for "the most obvious contradictions which underlie every contention and every enmity, concern the just, the beautiful and the good" (143). Yet Strauss thinks a phenomenological analysis of human λόγοι about the good can reveal the truth beyond their contradictoriness:

> All say of the good that they really wish it. That means that they want the truly good and not merely the appearance of good, and further they wish it; they pursue it, they desire it, they know, therefore, that they lack it, and that it is external to them.... Now a moment's reflection shows that what men usually conceive of as good – wealth, honours, and so forth – is not the same good as they *mean*; for they *mean* by "good" what is in every respect the contrary of evil, that which is completely free from evil. (PPH, 143–44; my emphasis)

---

[17] Ciccarelli (2020, 196) interprets this phenomenologically: "Strauss transforms, or enlarges, Husserlian intentional consciousness into linguistic-doxastic intentionality."

The intentionality of human speech thus points to nothing less than Platonic Forms and to their transcendence.[18] Concretely, the analysis of λόγοι that allows this hidden truth to emerge takes the form of a dialectic purification. But such cross-examination inevitably destabilizes the opinions from which it starts. And this puts the dialectician in a precarious position among her fellow citizens. The philosopher cannot simply deconstruct the doxastic foundations of her political community and leave it in ruins. That would be both unjust to the people who will not benefit from philosophical inquiry and dangerous for the philosophers themselves. The philosopher must therefore conduct her inquiry in a way that will preserve the appearance of a harmonious relationship between philosophers and "the unphilosophic many" (PPH, 147) by concealing the real tension between philosophy and unexamined opinions. How can a philosopher disclose the genuine nature of her activity to some and conceal it to others? Strauss thinks Plato's answer is simple: irony. To characterize irony chiefly as a kind of dissimulation, he follows both the original meaning of the word εἰρωνεία and Aristotle's discussion of irony in *NE* IV 7:

> Irony is a kind of dissimulation, or of untruthfulness. Aristotle therefore treats the habit of irony primarily as a vice. Yet irony is the dissembling, not of evil actions or of vices, but rather of good actions or of virtues; the ironic man, in opposition to the boaster, understates his worth. ... Irony is then the noble dissimulation of one's worth, of one's superiority. We may say, it is the humanity peculiar to the superior man: he spares the feelings of his inferiors by not displaying his superiority. (CM, 51)

Irony reveals to those who can recognize and understand it, and conceals to those who cannot. Thus, irony by its very nature discriminates between different kind of interlocutors. It obliquely shows the radical character of philosophical inquiry only to those who are more likely to be sympathetic to it. According to Strauss, ironic speech is therefore central to Platonic philosophical discourse, for it alleviates the precarious position of the philosopher in her city. By speaking differently to those who are sensitive to irony and to those who are not, irony also proves to be a powerful tool to overcome the defects of written speech as identified in the *Phaedrus*. Strauss most emphatically thinks of Platonic dialogues (and not just Socrates' speeches in these dialogues) as deeply ironic compositions.

In terms of Strauss' confrontation with Heidegger, there are two implications to draw from the ironic and dissimulative character of Plato's writings. First, this construal of irony entails that the interpreter's *Weg* is structurally similar than that of Heidegger's *Destruktion*. Indeed, the Straussian reader too must

---

[18] See especially PPH, 142. Compare NRH, 123–24.

attempt to decipher what remains unsaid by a serious rumination of what is explicitly said. However, Strauss' hypothesis of ironic writing (and the sociopolitical background that putatively makes such dissimulative writing necessary) comes along with the hypothesis that what truly matters and remains unsaid in a thinker's work is not unsaid because it is unthought. One could say that, rather, it is *precisely* because it is well thought through that it must remain unsaid. Strauss' hermeneutics of the unsaid then does not uncover unthought background theses or doctrines. This is indeed impossible for, as we shall see, Strauss thinks that the unsaid core of philosophical thinking is interrogative, not assertive; it is constituted of questions, not answers.[19]

Second, the tension between opinion and dialectical inquiry, which parallels the tension between the philosophers and "unphilosophic many," sheds some light on Strauss' Platonic position concerning what Heidegger calls *das Man* and *Gerede*. His position is quite different that the position we find in *Sein und Zeit*. First, Heidegger is skeptical that an inquiry *through* idle talk can be disclosive, and rather thinks that the only way to escape it is silence (*Schweigen*, see SZ, 273, 277, 296). Second, it is quite clear that Heidegger regards the tranquilizing character of *das Man* as a *problem* – that is, as an obstacle to Dasein's authentic self-uncovering. Heidegger unlikely thinks each and every person is able to escape the tranquility of the "They," and he does not present anxiety as an attunement that Dasein should encourage or try to provoke in the life of others.[20] Yet he does not seem to think, like Strauss' Plato, that the numbing effects of *Gerede* might be salutary for some. Thus, Heidegger has no interest and preserving it from destabilization, to say nothing of actually prescribing it for those who could not handle the experience resulting from *das Man*'s collapsing into meaninglessness. Compared to Strauss, Heidegger is not bothered by the political situation of the philosopher and the threat of persecution. To the latter, the concrete ethical-political facticity of human beings is of little interest.

More fundamentally, however, Heidegger would resist attempts to compare the experience of *Angst* to the experience resulting from the dialectic deconstruction of the basic opinions that hold the city together. In fact, Heidegger thinks that in destroying δόξα, the Platonic philosopher is not exposing herself to anything like the extreme disorientation experienced in anxiety; she is rather ascending to

---

[19] This is the most important point of contrast between esotericism as construed by Strauss and the Tübingen School. As Trabattoni (2009, 196) aptly explained, Strauss thinks that the apparent doctrines are exoteric and the questions underlying these doctrines are the esoteric core, while the Tubingen school thinks that the doctrinal teaching is hidden and esoteric, barely perceivable in what is explicitly said in the dialogues.

[20] It is also unclear that this would be at all possible: *Stimmungen* might be contagious and so in some sense "sharable," but they certainly are not at our disposal.

Forms. For Heidegger, the dialectic ascent to Forms is not genuinely equivalent to relinquishing the tranquilizing character of average inauthentic everydayness, for, as we have seen, he thinks of Forms as Plato's metaphysics of presence. And for Heidegger, thinking of being as presence, as static unchanging self-sameness, is a way to conceive of Being as essentially at our disposal and as potentially subject to our mastery and control. In other words, Plato's alleged metaphysics of presence is also dulling and tranquilizing. But this interpretation is absolutely incompatible with Strauss' understanding of Platonic Forms.

2.2 Platonic Forms as Perennial Questions

Since Aristotle, Plato's Forms have been criticized as an implausible and unnecessary metaphysical doctrine. Strauss, however, thinks Platonic Forms represent a phenomenologically sound hypothesis that derives naturally from our pretheoretical experience of the world. The world is given to us as pre-articulated according to different kinds or types of beings. It is of course possible to deny this prearticulated givenness as illusory. One can instead claim that Being is fundamentally One, and that the perceived plurality is an illusion that leads us astray (as per some interpretations of Parmenides). Strauss calls this noetic homogeneity. One can also claim that these formal differences only hide a common empirical structure reducible to a certain number of fundamental elements (as some materialist doctrines like atomism would suggest). Strauss calls this empirical heterogeneity. Plato's Socrates, he thinks, trusts the distinctive differences of the world as it appears to natural consciousness and thus embraces noetic heterogeneity:

> The discovery of noetic heterogeneity permits one to let things be what they are and takes away the compulsion to reduce essential differences to something common. The discovery of noetic heterogeneity means the vindication of what one could call common sense. ... Socrates discovered the paradoxical fact that, in a way, the most important truth is the most obvious truth, or the truth of the surface. (RCPR, 142)

But this hardly explains why Forms should transcend the perceptible world. Importantly, Strauss does not think that Forms are identical with the kinds and shapes into which the world is perceptually articulated; rather, noetic heterogeneity prompts the notion of or leads toward Forms. But Forms are not the *answer* to the question prompted by noetic heterogeneity: "the 'idea' of the thing is that which we mean *by trying to find out* the 'what' or the 'nature' of a thing or a class of things" (HPP, 54; my emphasis). Forms are not identical to things' natures. They are what we are trying to find out. Socrates, Strauss says, "viewed man in light of the *unchanging ideas, i.e. of the fundamental and permanent problems*"

(WIPP, 39; my emphasis). Socratic philosophy "is knowledge that one does not know; that is to say, it is knowledge of what one does not know, or *awareness of the fundamental problems* and, therewith, of the fundamental alternatives regarding their solution that are coeval with human thought" (NRH, 32; my emphasis). Platonic Forms are here interpreted as questions and problems and not as answers or solutions. On this reading, the Form or Idea of Justice, for instance, would be the same as the question or the problem of justice. This means that to grasp the Form of Justice is equivalent to grasping the question "what is justice?" in all its problematicity. This is not to say that Forms are mere contentless question marks. For truly understanding a question is only possible, as Strauss indicates, if we are aware of at least some of its potential solutions.

In different times and places, these solutions may vary. But "the fundamental problems, such as the problem of justice, persist or retain their identity in all historical change" (NRH, 32). In this very sense, Platonic Forms do in fact transcend the sensible world. Strauss' interpretation of Forms as perennial problems offers a twofold response to Heidegger. First, it challenges Heidegger's view that the way in which Plato answered the question of Being initiated the oblivion of that very question. If Plato understood Being in terms of the Forms and Forms as problems and questions, we seem indeed far away from an understanding of Being as presence. In fact, any metaphysics of presence supposes that the question of being has been in some sense *answered*, albeit implicitly and unwittingly. But according to Strauss, Socratic-Platonic philosophy, insofar as it is *zetetic* and not dogmatic, precisely refuses to provide such an answer. Philosophy

> is neither dogmatic nor skeptic, and still less "decisionist," but zetetic (or skeptic in the original sense of the term). Philosophy as such is nothing but genuine awareness of the problems, i.e., of the fundamental and comprehensive problems. It is impossible to think about these problems without becoming inclined toward a solution, toward one or the other of the very few typical solutions. Yet as long as there is no wisdom but only quest for wisdom, the evidence of all solutions is necessarily smaller than the evidence of the problems. (OT, 196)[21]

Second, Strauss' interpretation offers a resistance to Heidegger's attempt to think Being temporally and historically. This is indeed a crucial aspect of Strauss's lifelong struggle with Heidegger as "the radical historicist" who threatens the very possibility of philosophy. Strauss' zetetic resistance to time and history consists in affirming the self-sameness of fundamental questions

---

[21] On the zetetic character of Strauss' recovery of Plato, see especially Tanguay (2007, 86–92, 108, 123–30, 147, 180–92) and Velkley (2011, 113, 161–62). On zetetic Platonism as a response to Heidegger, see Fried (2021).

across historical changes. But from a Heideggerian standpoint, would not this insistence on persistence and identity over and against change and difference be a sign that the zetetic solution answers the question of Being *implicitly* in favor of constant presence? Is the affirmation of ahistorical problems not some avatar of the metaphysics of presence? Had Strauss really thought of these problems and questions as eternal, that could very well be the case. (It should, however, be noted that the *Seinsweise* of questions, insofar as they are fundamental and genuinely experienced as such, cannot be presence-at-hand: eternal questions could perhaps betray presence as *Anwesenheit*, but certainly not as *Vorhandenheit*).[22] Yet the fact that Strauss does not call these problems eternal but rather "coeval with human thought" makes the case more difficult. For in a lecture on Heidegger, Strauss claimed that saying that something is "coeval with man" implies that it is "not sempiternal or eternal" (RCPR, 45–46). This would mean that while Strauss denies that Forms as questions change across *human history*, he obliquely recognizes some kind of emergence, some kind of inaugural event thanks to which the question of Being arose. But would that not suggest a deeper affinity between Strauss and Heidegger than is usually recognized? Yes and no. While Strauss' meditations on the elusiveness of Being indeed bring him quite close to Heidegger, his claim that *Plato* thought of Being in this way again suggests a picture of Platonism that strikingly differs from Heidegger's critical depiction.

2.3 Being and the Elusiveness of the Whole

In 1946, Strauss wrote that Plato's dialogical compositions preclude the possibility of reading them like treatises from which we could extract doctrinal content: "Plato composed his writings in such a way as to prevent for all time their use as authoritative texts. His dialogues supply us not so much with an answer to the riddle of being as with a most articulate 'imitation' of that riddle. His teaching can never become the subject of indoctrination" (ONIPP, 351). Strauss does not mean that Plato has a solution to the question of Being and simply refuses to communicate it to his readers. Instead, he thinks Plato offers no solution to the question and emphasizes that philosophy should see that and why it cannot reach such solution. Strauss will reiterate this view several times, albeit in slightly different formulations. In later writings, the "riddle of being" becomes the cosmological question of "the whole." In "What Is Political Philosophy?" he claims: "Socrates was so far from being committed to a specific cosmology that his knowledge was knowledge

---

[22] Nor are fundamental problems and questions ready-to-hand (*zuhanden*) in the way tools are: they much more likely belong to Dasein's structure as care (*Sorge*), and not merely to pragmatic preoccupation (*Besorgen*).

of ignorance. Knowledge of ignorance is not ignorance. It is knowledge of the elusive character of the truth, of the whole. Socrates, then, viewed man in light of the mysterious character of the whole" (WIPP, 38–39).

In *The City and Man*, he speaks again of the "elusiveness of the whole" (CM, 21) and reasserts his view that Plato's writings imitate that elusiveness. And there is little doubt that what is at issue here is the question of Being:

> Plato's work consists of many dialogues because it imitates the manyness, the variety, the heterogeneity of being. The many dialogues form a *kosmos* which mysteriously imitates the mysterious *kosmos*. The Platonic *kosmos* imitates or reproduces its model in order to awaken us to the mystery of the model and to assist us in articulating that mystery. (CM, 60–61)

Strauss' articulation of such mystery is only schematic and formal, but helpful nonetheless. Key here is the idea that Being as a whole is composed of many parts. If this is so, our approach to Being will inevitably take the form of the hermeneutic circle of parts and whole: we can only know the whole if we can know all of its parts (cf. NRH, 122), but we can only truly know each part if we know its position and function within that whole. But this in turn requires a knowledge of the whole. This does not entail that we have no access to the whole whatsoever: "The whole eludes us but we know parts: we possess partial knowledge of parts" (WIPP, 39). The whole rather reveals itself to us partly through partial access to its parts – that is, it reveals itself precisely insofar as it eludes us. For Strauss, this state of affairs once more implies that the *question* of Being has priority over any potential answer to that question:

> "The elusiveness of the whole necessarily affects the knowledge of every part. Because of the elusiveness of the whole, the beginning or the questions retain a greater evidence than the end or the answers; return to the beginning remains a constant necessity" (CM, 21).

Insofar as it emphasizes the questioning at the expense of any eventual solution, Strauss' thesis concerning the elusiveness of Being in Platonic philosophy brings him and his Plato quite close to Heidegger. Heidegger in fact famously wrote that "questioning is the piety of thinking" (GA 7, 36). Likewise, in the *Origin of the Work of Art*, he says that "every answer remains powerful as an answer so long as it is rooted in the questioning" (GA 5, 58). Yet Strauss thinks this Socratic-Platonic priority of the question is radically unmodern (CM, 20–21).

Since for Heidegger Platonism as metaphysics is the forerunner of this modern philosophical-scientific attitude, Strauss' Plato here appears much closer to Heidegger himself than to Heidegger's Plato. Similarly, Strauss' analysis of the alleged Platonic awareness of the fundamental elusiveness of

Being makes his Plato sympathetic to Heidegger. For both Strauss' Plato and Heidegger, Being reveals itself only partially and mysteriously – that is, in its concealment.[23] Truth is therefore never full disclosedness: ἀλήθεια is always bound with and blurred by λήθη, an interweaving that the dialogical and ironic compositions of Plato's dialogues, Strauss thinks, imitates.[24] It is true that Heidegger does not provide the kind of mereological argument that Strauss seems especially fond of when addressing Being's elusiveness. Although he at times seems to pose the question of Being in terms of wholeness (e.g. GA 40, 4), he is clearly skeptical that going through each part of that whole would be in any way helpful.[25] But neither does Strauss think that the mystery of the whole can be resolved by turning to its parts. The point is precisely that a whole is not reducible to the sum of its parts and hence always eludes attempts to grasp it qua whole. Particular beings or entities (*Seienden*) show themselves to us qua entities, but in doing so, they conceal themselves "as a whole and as such." Thus, Strauss' Plato seems to agree with Heidegger on the fundamental point, namely that the whole is ultimately elusive, fundamentally hidden or concealed (cf. e.g. GA 9, 193).

We may finally push the question a bit further and ask whether Strauss' Plato's way of posing the question of Being might not be, for Heidegger, flawed from the very start. By interrogating Being via the question of the whole, are we not understanding it in terms of the parts that make up that whole? Are we thereby not understanding Being in terms of beings, *Sein* in terms of *das Seiende*? Such a confusion of the question of Being with the question of a being, however supreme that being may be, is the running thread of metaphysics in its ontotheological constitution, and it is quite clear that Heidegger ultimately identifies Platonic ontology with such ontotheology (cf. GA 11, 73; cf. GA 15, 435–36). Even the introduction of the notion of the beings as a whole might fail in avoiding this problem. Heidegger says that metaphysics does not even *ask* the question of the truth of Being because "it thinks Being only by signifying beings as beings (*das Seiende als das Seiende*). It means beings as a whole (*das Seiende im Ganzen*) and speaks of Being. It states Being and means beings as beings (*das Seiende als das Seiende*)" (GA 9, 370) I see two potential responses to this worry.

First, Strauss seems aware of the risk of misconstruing the whole as just a higher kind of being (*Seiende*) This is why he explicitly says that "the whole

---

[23] Taminiaux (2002, 214–15) too sees this as a debt of Strauss to Heidegger.
[24] Benardete (2000, 409) is to my knowledge the first to have perceived that logographic esotericism in Strauss parallels and points to a "metaphysical esotericism."
[25] On mereology and Dasein's (not Being's) wholeness see SZ, 244n1, Øverenget (1996), McManus (2016, 181–88) and Rojcewicz (2021, 15–19 and 31–36, 114)

cannot 'be' in the same sense in which everything that is 'something' 'is': the whole must be 'beyond being'" (NRH, 122). Note that Strauss here keenly uses scare quotes to differentiate the way in which the whole and its parts "are." With this reference to Plato's ἐπέκεινα τῆς οὐσίας, *Resp.* 509b9), he intends to demarcate precisely the whole from any entity, any *Seiende*. In other words, in the hiatus that separates the whole from its parts, Strauss seems to see Heidegger's ontological difference, the difference between *Sein* and *das Seiende*. Most intriguingly, Strauss implicitly identifies the whole with Plato's Idea of the Good. This is an unusual interpretation, as more standard or orthodox interpretations would rather see in the Good the principle or cause of the Platonic cosmos. But these interpretations naturally yield the view that the Idea of the Good is the supreme being that supervenes the whole of beings, and so the picture of Platonic ontology they provide is the perfect target of Heidegger's accusation of ontotheology. Not only does Strauss' unorthodox interpretation have the advantage of dodging that accusation, but its emphasis on the "beyond" brings his Plato close to some of Heidegger's early approach to the *Seinsfrage*. In fact, while Heidegger's 1940 interpretation of Plato construes the Idea of the Good in ontotheological terms, he claims in 1927 that "what we are seeking is the ἐπέκεινα τῆς οὐσίας" (GA 24, 404). And in *Being and Time*, he asserts: "Being is the absolutely transcendent (*Sein ist das transcendens schlechthin*)" (SZ, 38).[26]

Second, according to Strauss's interpretation of Platonic ontology, there is hardly a risk of falling back on an understanding of beings instead of Being because Platonic Forms are understood not as immaterial substances or supernatural entities but as fundamental questions or problems. By emphasizing the problematicity and the questionability of Being, Strauss' Plato is far from embracing a tranquilizing ontotheology or metaphysics of presence. Strauss' zetetic Platonism is not metaphysical in any Heideggerian sense.

3 Gadamer's Dialogical Platonism

In his 1973 *Selbstdarstellung*, Gadamer said that, for a long time, he always had the "damned feeling (*verdammte Gefühl*)" that Heidegger was looking over his shoulder (GW2, 491). Unsurprisingly, most of his explicit critiques of Heidegger were only published after Heidegger's death. Nonetheless, even Gadamer's early writings show that he is implicitly distancing himself from his master, especially concerning Plato. Notably, they differ in their respective

---

[26] Thus Ralkowski (2009, 63, 75–85) claims that the genuine desideratum of Heidegger's inquiry is, despite Heidegger's critique of Plato, the Idea of the Good properly understood. For a different reading of the compatibility between the Idea of the Good and Heidegger (through the question of normativity), see Crowell (2013, 30, 187, 223, and 277).

understandings of the relation between Plato and Aristotle, and this difference helps explain how Gadamer is able to free himself from his master's interpretation of Plato. To see what this difference entails, we may look at how Gadamer frames the argument of his *Habilitationschrift* and compare it to the structure of Heidegger's 1924–25 *Sophist* lectures.[27]

In both texts, Aristotle serves as the entry point into Plato. In both cases, this Aristotelian detour toward Plato is justified by the "old principle of hermeneutics" according to which we should "proceed from the clear into the obscure," and the view that Aristotle developed Platonic insights with greater conceptual clarity (GA 19, 11–12 and PDE, 7). For Heidegger, the alleged obscurity of Plato's is connected with the (Aristotelian) view that dialectic is merely "attemptive (πειραστική)"[28] and thus does not have the means to reach its goal (see e.g. GA 19, 197). For Gadamer, however, this tentativeness or provisional character (*Vorläufigkeit*) is not a defect of Platonic dialectic. Rather, it reflects philosophical depth. Thus, unlike his master, Gadamer claims that Aristotle's conceptual clarification of Plato involves a form of restriction (*Einschränkung*). He further claims that this Aristotelian limitation or restriction is rooted in a deeper existential attitude which *Being and Time* would describe as inauthentic, namely Dasein's "original (*ursprüngliche*) tendency toward knowledge as a removal of all disconcerting unfamiliarity (*als Aufhebung aller befremdenden Unvertrautheit*)" (FDE 22; GW 5, 18; trans. modif.). Platonic philosophy is not obscure: its form is simply more attuned to the uncanniness and unfamiliarity characteristic of human finite existence. Aristotle's conceptual work may be clearer, more scientific, but this advantage comes at a cost: by canceling out what remains unfamiliar and unknown in it, it does violence to the phenomenon of human life. Already early on, the young Gadamer is significantly departing from Heidegger's interpretation: Aristotelian scientific treatises do *not* represent an advance compared to Plato's dialogues. In 1930, Gadamer most sharply contrasts Aristotle's "clarity of the concept (*Klarheit des Begriffs*)" with Platonic thinking as an emphatically *living* activity:

> But in its world-historical form, the fate of philosophy is for the first time visible with Aristotle: the form of life, which had painted itself in grey with the greyness of the concept, had gotten old and could not rejuvenate itself, but only know. Therein Aristotle and the beginning of philosophy differentiate themselves from the dialogical dialectic of Plato. (GW 5, 248; my trans.)

---

[27] Gadamer acknowledges the influence of Heidegger's lectures on Aristotle in *Plato's Dialectical Ethics* (PDE, xxxii).
[28] *Met.* 1004b25; *Soph. el.* 169b24–25, 171b4, 171b9, 172a21–22, 172a28, 183b1.

Thus Gadamer's preference for Plato over Aristotle, which allows his first self-distancing from Heidegger's reading of Greek philosophy, is anchored in his deep appreciation for the dialogical character of Platonic thinking.

3.1 Dialogue and the Ethical Character of the Hermeneutical Situation

It is therefore not surprising that the thrust of Gadamer's approach to the *Philebus* in 1931 is a reflection on the meaning of Platonic dialectic as embedded in human dialogue: "the theory of *dialectic*, in Plato, is the theory of the possibility of *dialogue*" (PDE, xxv). Rejecting the developmentalist approach to Plato, Gadamer says: "the theory of dialectic must be grasped on the basis of the concrete situation of coming to a shared understanding (*Verständigung*) ... all inquiry regarding a change and development in Plato's dialectic is secondary and must itself get its orientation from the genesis of dialectic from dialogue" (PDE, 113).

His account of dialectic and dialogue takes the form of a phenomenological analysis of the intersubjective conditions of the possibility of coming to an understanding (*Verständigung*). Understanding philosophical inquiry as "a specific way in which the care of being-in-the-world is put into effect (*ein eigentümlicher Vollzugscharakter der Sorge des In-der-Welt-seins*)" (PDE, 27), Gadamer builds on several of Heidegger's fundamental-ontological insights, but pushes them further in directions that Heidegger himself did not explore. Most significantly, his interpretation departs from Heidegger by emphasizing the ethical dimension of dialogical inquiry and thereby recognizing authentic possibilities within shared, communal speech.

Gadamer understands speech primordially as "communal having to do (*gemeinsamen Zutunhaben*) with something" (PDE, 29). Each component of this phrase plays an important role in Gadamer's interpretation. First, speech is shared and common; it points to a dialogical community and is never solipsistic or monological. Second, speech not only occurs within human action, but it itself *is* a kind of action (*Tun*), a way of actively concerning oneself with something. Third, this "with something" indicates that speech is always intentional in the Husserlian sense: it is always directed toward something, which Gadamer calls and thinks of as a *Sache*, not an indifferent thing, but some thing or subject matter that is *at issue* and *matters* for the interlocutors.

On the first point, Gadamer is subtly but surely rejecting Heidegger's analysis of λόγος and *Rede* in both the *Sophist* lectures and *Being and Time*. In the former, Heidegger's critique of Platonic dialectic relies on an interpretation of λόγος wherein speech "is primarily idle talk (*Gerede*)," and therefore concealing (*verdeckend*) (GA 19, 197). In the latter, idle talk is also the falling tendency of *Rede* par excellence, and *especially* of *Rede* amidst the most predominant form of *Mitsein*, namely *das Man*. It is thus no surprise that the call of conscience (*Gewissen*) which alone is able to bring Dasein back to its own self takes the form of a silencing (*Schweigen*) (SZ, 273, 277, 296). By emphasizing the dialogical character of language, Gadamer's Platonism is a rejoinder to Heidegger's analysis of *Rede*.

The idea that dialectic is an expression of being-in-the-world as concerned comportment echoes Heidegger's view that our primary encounter with innerworldly beings is a practical engagement with πράγματα. Like Strauss, however, Gadamer rejects Heidegger's interpretation of πράγματα as tools and therewith his analysis of everyday facticity in terms of the work world (*Weltwerk*). In this regard, he emphasizes Aristotle's distinction between ποίησις and πρᾶξις, and reads it back into his account of the dialogical community, where φρόνησις, not τέχνη, serves as guide (see e.g. PDE 89–90, cf. IG, 46).[29] Of course, Heidegger had magisterially interpreted that distinction and emphasized its importance in the *Sophist* lectures, but Gadamer implicitly rejects Heidegger's hyper-ontologizing interpretation of φρόνησις, where the autotelic character of its "uncovering (ἀληθεύειν)" is assimilated to Dasein's self-disclosure in *Gewissen* (see GA 19, 48–57). For Gadamer, such ontologized πρᾶξις is a denatured πρᾶξις because it is entirely devoid of any concrete ethical-political meaning. He thinks that Plato's dialogues depict human situatedness as practical, but that this facticity is thoroughly ethical in a more ordinary sense: "All Dasein lives continually in an understanding of aretē [virtue]" (PDE, 53).

Gadamer's anti-Heideggerian reappraisal of ethical facticity in Plato is not for that matter oblivious of Heidegger's sensitivity to the constant threat of fallenness. It is not so much that Gadamer evades the problem of inauthentic modes of speech, but that he thinks Plato too was acutely aware of this problem. In his 1931 *Platonbuch*, Gadamer devotes a lengthy analysis of the distinction between "successful forms (*Vollzugsformen*)" and "fallen forms (*Verfallsformen*)" of language. This distinction accounts for the difference between dialectic and genuine dialogue on the one hand, and eristics and sophistry on the other hand. According to Gadamer's Plato, the source of fallen forms of speech is an ethical vice: φθόνος (ill will, malice, envy). What is interesting with this analysis of φθόνος is that this disposition appears *both* as morally vicious *and* as ontologically obstructive: "*Phthonos* ... means concerns about being ahead of others or not being left behind by others. As such, its effect in conversation is to cause an apprehensive holding back from

---

[29] See also GW 1, 317–29.

talk that presses toward discovering the true state of affairs (*Sachverhalts*)" (PDE, 44–45). Therefore, authentic speech is possible in a community where interlocutors are genuinely concerned with *virtue* and are thus ἄφθονος. Gadamer's interpretation of the Platonic critique of φθόνος yields several ethical aspects of what good hermeneutic dispositions look like in *Truth and Method*. Being ἄφθονος means not to try to win the argument at all cost (using eristic techniques such as "refutation for the sake of refutation"), and to be genuinely open that we might actually be able to learn something from our interlocutors. It also means that we are willing to speak our thoughts transparently and submit them sincerely to common cross-examination, and that we can reasonably expect that our interlocutors do the same. Above all, it means a disposition wholly devoted to understanding the *Sache*, the subject matter at issue in the dialogue. Strikingly, Gadamer here replaces Heidegger's solipsistic *Sein zum Tode* with a communal, dialogical *Sein zur Sache* (GW 5, 24; PDE, 32). This transformation is more than a change from the individual to the interpersonal: it represents an *ethical* response to Heidegger's fundamental-ontological worry.

Another way in which speech and action are tied together in Gadamer's Plato is the structural form of Socratic-Platonic conversations. As the emphasis on the ethical character of the dialogical situation should have made clear, dialogues are not mere speeches. They are speeches spoken by particular persons with particular intellectual and ethical dispositions in particular settings or circumstances. As lived conversations, dialogues are thus a complex mixture of speech and action, of λόγος and ἔργον (cf. PTI, 10). In the *Laches*, Socrates tells Laches that since he is courageous in his deeds without being able to define courage, he lacks the "doric harmony" between λόγος and ἔργον (193d11–e4). Gadamer contends that Socratic dialogues in general aim precisely at this harmony (DD, 2–3). Within the dialogues, the inquiry is not just meant to allow an understanding of the *Sache* to emerge, but to transform the interlocutors' lives accordingly, to make their existences more harmonious by attuning their speeches to their deeds, and vice versa.

Gadamer thinks this principle is also true at the extra-dialogical level, namely in *our* conversations with Plato's dialogues. Fulfilling this principle is a difficult task, especially since what Socrates says and what Plato writes are not the same thing. Following (like Strauss) Paul Friedländer's approach to the dramatic construction of the dialogues, Gadamer thinks that interpreting the Platonic dialogues requires that we disentangle their complex interweaving of λόγος and ἔργον (cf. DD, 6). This in turn means that we can never abstract particular λόγοι from Plato's compositions and attribute it to him as a Platonic teaching. If this is so, then the implication is that the site of truth for Plato is not λόγος, but the activity of the dialogue as a whole, its movement between λόγος and ἔργον. In this respect, we may say that Gadamer's Plato anticipates Heidegger's critique of the logical prejudice of metaphysics, which is at play in Heidegger's interpretation of the transformation of truth in Plato: between λόγος and ἔργον, truth is not propositional.[30] But much more generally, Gadamer's principle of Platonic hermeneutics short-circuits most if not all of Heidegger's attempts to extract Platonic doctrines from the dialogues: "The literary form of the dialogue places language and concept back within the original movement of the conversation. This protects words from all dogmatic abuse (*gegen allen dogmatischen Mißbrauch*)" (TM 377; GW 1, 374). In light of this, Heidegger's insensitivity to the dialogical form of Plato's writings is the sine qua non condition of his interpretation of Platonism as metaphysics.[31] This may be why Gadamer said that Heidegger could not access properly the "*Denkgeschehen* of the Platonic dialogues" (GW 3, 289).

3.2 The Forms between Plato and Aristotle

His rejection of dogmatic interpretations notwithstanding, Gadamer does think that Forms are crucial to Plato's philosophy, but he interprets them in a radically unorthodox way. He in fact most explicitly denies the somewhat standard two-world Platonism: "Plato was no Platonist who taught the two worlds [doctrine]" (GW 7, 331, cf. PTI, 9). Gadamer likes to recall that Plato's *Parmenides* voices objections to the separation of Forms that anticipate the core of Aristotle's critique of Platonism (e.g. GW 7, 344). And since Gadamer rejects the developmentalist approach to the study of the *corpus platonicum*, he does not think we should or even can ascribe this self-critique to a more "mature" Plato who has abandoned the Forms and replaced them with a new ontology (e.g. the four great kinds of the *Sophist* or the Limit and the Unlimited of the *Philebus*). As we shall see, he rather thinks that this putatively "late ontology" is shedding light on the Forms and help us understand them better rather than replacing them, and the *Parmenides* does not represent a disavowal of the Forms but is rather compatible with them. This is why Gadamer paradoxically maintains that one can hold *both* Platonic Forms *and* Aristotle's critique thereof: "After all, it could be that the Aristotelian critique [of Plato] – like many a critique – is right indeed in what it says, but not as to who against whom it says it" (GW 2, 424). Gadamer follows Aristotle in rejecting the χωρισμός and rather emphasizes the participatory dynamic of Forms.

---

[30] On Heidegger and the "logical prejudice" of metaphysics, see Dahlstrom (2001).
[31] A point especially well made by Hyland (2004, 17–83).

In order to understand this participatory dynamic properly, we need to examine what Gadamer sees as the paradigm or model of Platonic ontology: whereas Aristotle guides himself according to the *"insight into the nature of what lives," "in Plato it is obviously the insight into the nature of number which supports and directs his thinking and conceptualization"* (DD, 200). The paradigm of number is so important that he sometimes calls Platonic metaphysics "metamathematics" (GW 7, 280). But this mathematical orientation does not foreshadow anything like what Heidegger will criticize as calculative thinking. The two crucial features of the arithmetic structure of Platonic Forms rather point to (1) an account of the natural articulation of the world as phenomenologically experienced; and (2) the "radical participation" of Forms with each other, which indicates a dynamic ontology wherein Being is understood fundamentally as relation.

It is his friend Jacob Klein who convinced Gadamer of the importance of the mathematical paradigm.[32] In *Die griechische Logistik und die Entstehung der Algebra* (1934–36), Klein argued that Platonic Forms ought to be understood in light of Aristotle's critique of the ideal numbers or εἰδητικοὶ ἀριθμοί in *Metaphysics* A, M, and N. Aristotle informs us that the two most fundamental principles of this theory are the One and the indefinite Dyad. For Klein, these two principles are the defining moments of the "arithmos structure," a structure that plays out most relevantly in a nonmathematical way in the Eleatic Stranger's introduction of the μέγιστα γένη in the *Sophist*.[33] Before dealing with the relations amidst Forms themselves, let us first pay attention to the second point highlighted by Klein, namely how the One and Dyad are at work in "every possible articulation." Klein connected the One with rest (στάσις) and self-sameness or identity (ταὐτόν) and the Dyad with otherness (θάτερον) and motion (κίνησις) in the *Sophist*. Gadamer agrees and further associates the One and the Dyad with the notions of the Limit (πέρας) and the Unlimited (ἄπειρον) in the *Philebus*. Gadamer says that from the One and the indefinite Dyad just like from the πέρας-ἄπειρον "all numbers just as all beings in general are derived" (GW 7, 215, 156–57).

In what sense do all beings (*Seiende*) derive, like numbers, from these principles? Key to understanding this claim is the Greek concept of number as a *definite or delimited plurality*.[34] A definite plurality is not a mere manifold,

---

[32] And not the Tubingen school. On Klein's influence on Gadamer's interpretation, see GW 5, 159, DD, 129, Zuckert (1996, 96), and Renaud (2019, 356–57). On Gadamer and the Tubingen school, see Grondin (2010).

[33] Klein (1992, 92).

[34] On such an understanding of number, see Klein (1992, 46–60) and Aristotle, *Met.* I1.1035a30; I6.1056b23–24; N1.1088a5.

but rather a plurality of such and such entities. The delimitation of this plurality is possible thanks to a unit or monad (μόνας) that makes counting *in each case* possible. Thus, for Greek arithmetics, numbers are primarily *counting* numbers: I can count the five horses in the field thanks to the unit "horse," which delimits the manifold that gives itself to me perceptually.[35] The world as it is phenomenologically experienced by natural consciousness is always an interweaving of sameness and otherness, a mixture of πέρας and ἄπειρον. As Gadamer puts it in *Truth and Method*, "seeing means articulating (*Sehen heißt aufgliedern*)" (GW 1, 97). But this articulated character of the world as a mixture of manifold and unity is not just a function of perception; for Gadamer, it is chiefly the function of language, for it is λόγος that has an "*arithmos* structure" (DD, 129).[36] Like with Strauss' notion of noetic heterogeneity, then, Platonic Forms here delimit the manifoldness of the world much like the Aristotelian εἰδή do.[37] Dialectic, as an "art of differentiating (IG, 95 ; GW 7, 180)," moves further in the same direction as the pretheoretical (linguistic-perceptual) awareness of the articulation of the world, and is thus able to recognize that all beings "derive from" – that is, are made manifest and disclosed by the One and the indefinite Dyad.

This account of the function of Forms seems compatible with what Heidegger says about the Platonic ἰδέα as what lets see the Being of beings (e.g. GA 34, 48–50).[38] But for Heidegger, what is crucial is that the Idea displays the *presence* of the Being of beings for a beholder, and so putatively betrays Plato's commitment to the view that Being chiefly means presence. While it will be clearer in the foregoing analyses and especially in Section 3.3 why Gadamer's interpretation of Platonic Forms rejects Heidegger's criticism, it is worth considering here how Gadamer is already in a position to respond to this accusation. The crucial point is that Gadamer thinks that Plato's *Sophist* proposes to think of Being as a community or interweaving of motion and rest, self-sameness and difference, and being and nonbeing. This proposal is not to be understood as a hierarchical organization of the kinds wherein motion would be subordinated to rest, difference to sameness, and nonbeing to being. If these are really thought *together* and if this togetherness is indeed key to the γιγαντομαχία περὶ τῆς οὐσίας, then Plato certainly acknowledges the "other" of presence and does not reduce the meaning of Being to *Anwesenheit*.[39] While the principles of the One and indefinite Dyad may very well look like the kind of dogmatic metaphysics that Heidegger criticizes in Plato, Gadamer's account of that

---

[35] See also Zuckert (1996, 96–97).   [36] See also Renaud (2019, 363 and 369).
[37] See Lynch (2013).   [38] See Section 1.2.1.
[39] See Prufer's (1997, 549) excellent remark: "Two [i.e. the Dyad] protects the *lêthê* in *alêtheia* and thus prevents philosophy from degenerating into doctrine and pursuit of the honoring of doctrine. Gadamer reads Plato by using Heidegger's *Bergung* against Heidegger's reading of Plato."

teaching reveals a Plato altogether different than the one we meet in Heidegger's writings.

We may now turn to the second point and examine how the arithmetic model Gadamer embraces helps us understand the "radical participation" of Forms between each other. Gadamer claims that the paradigm according to which we ought to understand Forms is more specifically the sum number (DD, 132–34, 146, 208–9). The sum number is paradigmatic because it displays how an eidetic unit (the sum number itself) is always connected to other eidetic units (other numbers or the aforementioned monadic unit) in various ways through participation without being reducible to these constitutive units (cf. PTI, 9). Let us look at an example. The sum number 6 is related to 1 insofar as $6 = 1+1+1+1+1+1$, but it is also related to 2, 3, 4, and 5 insofar as $6 = 2+2+2 = 2+3+1 = 3+3 = 4+2 = 5+1$. The number 6 is irreducible to the sum of its constitutive eidetic units because 6 cannot be predicated of any of its parts, and because some properties of 6 are absent of some of its parts (e.g. 6 is even but the two 3s that compose it are odd) (DD, 132–33). The arithmetic model helps us see at once how Forms "participate into each other" while also being irreducible to one another. Thus, Gadamer's interpretation of participation exceeds by far the unidirectionality of the particular's participation in Forms that is usually at the center of the χωρισμός thesis. He thinks it is helpful in that respect to distinguish participation (μέθεξις) from imitation (μίμησις):

> When the stars bring the numbers to representation through their paths, we call this representation "mimesis" and take it to be an approximation of the genuine being (*Annäherung an das eigentlich Seiende*). In contrast to this, "methexis" is a wholly formal relationship of participation, based on mutuality (*Gegenseitigkeit*). "Mimesis" always points in the direction of that which one approaches. ... "Methexis", however, as the Greek μετά already signifies, implies that one thing is there together with something else (*daß es mit dem anderen zusammen da ist*). Participation, μεταλαμβάνειν, completes itself only in genuine being together and belonging together (*eigentlichen Zusammensein und Zusammengehören*), μετέχειν. (GW 7, 246; PP, 262; trans. modif.; my emphasis)

Such an interpretation of participation might do justice to the συμπλοκή, κοινωνία, and μίξις of the *Sophist* and the *Philebus* as ways of understanding the *mutual* relation between Forms or kinds themselves. However, we ought to note that if Gadamer thinks – *as he seems to* – that this applies to the relation between Forms and perceptible particulars too, emphasis on mutuality (*Gegenseitigkeit*) where we would expect transcendence (*Jenseitigkeit*) is extremely unorthodox. It in fact suggests that a Form *depends* on what partakes in it instead of being "itself by itself," αὐτὸ καθ' αὐτό. Likewise, if the particulars and Forms "are there together" (Gadamer also translates μέθεξις as *Mitdasein*), we may ask again how Platonic Forms differ from Aristotle's enmattered Form (ἔνυλον εἶδος).[40] This seeming immanentizing of Forms through reciprocity with particulars will play a structural role in Gadamer's interpretation of the Good and the Beautiful.

Before turning to that interpretation, we may ask once more how Gadamer's account so far responds to Heidegger's challenge. His understanding of the "radical participation" of Forms into each other attempts to think Being neither as a supernatural entity, nor as presence, but as a nexus of potential reciprocal relations. With his account of μέθεξις as *Mitdasein* and *Zusammensein*, Gadamer seems to be taking up what Heidegger had momentarily seen in his 1924–25 lectures before dropping it, namely that "to be with one another (*Miteinandersein*)" and "to be related to one another (*Aufeinanderbezogensein*)" might be the "meaning of Being (*Sinn von Sein*)" at the heart of Plato's *Sophist* (GA 19, 478–79). To be sure, Heidegger quickly reinterpreted this potential sense of Being as "copresence (*Mitanwesenheit*)," but from a Gadamerian perspective, this hardly does justice to the active dimension of "mixing" and of forming a community (κοινωνεῖν): copresence is not community and need not involve any mixing; at any rate, it certainly is no *genuine* belonging together (*eigentliche Zusammengehören*). Once more, there seems to be a primacy of πρᾶξις over ποίησις in Gadamer's Platonism. Thus, his interpretation of Platonic Forms does not betray a metaphysics of presence, and, as we shall now see, his understanding of the relation between the Good, the Beautiful, and truth runs directly against Heidegger's thesis concerning the transformation of the essence of truth in Plato.

3.3 The Elusiveness of the Good and the Priority of the Beautiful

Surely, one of the most difficult problems in interpreting Plato is what it means for the Idea of the Good to be "beyond Being (ἐπέκεινα τῆς οὐσίας, *Resp.*509b9)." The problem is all the more pressing for Gadamer, since his understanding of the Forms tends to minimize their transcendence in favor of their mutual relation with perceptible particulars that make up the phenomenal world. In *Truth and Method*, Gadamer claims that the radical transcendence of the Good entails its unknowability: it is absolutely ungraspable (*schlechthin ungreifbar*, GW 1, 484). In the *Idea of the Good in Platonic-Aristotelian Philosophy*, this ungraspability is further determined as a self-withdrawal: "'It itself,' αὐτὸ τὸ ἀγαθόν, withdraws itself (*entzieht sich*)." (GW 7, 198). Key to an understanding of this self-withdrawal of the Good is Gadamer's reading of the *Republic* passage in light of a passage of the *Philebus* where the Good is also

---

[40] I discuss this further in my Pageau-St-Hilaire (2024).

said to withdraw or "flee." Bracketing once more any potential developmentalist worry concerning this intertextual interpretation,[41] he asserts that

> [the ἐπέκεινα] is the mythical form in which Plato essentially expresses what he makes explicit in the *Philebus* when he says that the Good "appears" in the Beautiful (*daß dort das Gute im Schönen "erscheint"*) ... That is the meaning of the statement that the Good takes refuge in the Beautiful (*daß das Gute in dem Schönen seine Zuflucht nehme*). (GW 7, 198)

In light of Heidegger's critique of Platonism, it is crucial to note that in Gadamer's interpretation, the self-withdrawal of the Good is at once an appearing in the Beautiful. It is in virtue of its power to appear that Gadamer claims there is in Plato a "priority of the Beautiful (*Vorzug des Schönen*)" (GW 1, 484). Drawing here not just in the conjunction of the *Republic* and the *Philebus*, but importantly on the determination of the Beautiful as the "most appearing (ἐκφανέστατον)" Form in the *Phaedrus* (250d7), Gadamer is not merely interpreting Plato but appropriating his insights and incorporating them into his own conceptual articulation of hermeneutic truth:

> However closely Plato has linked the idea of the beautiful with that of the good, he is still aware of a difference between the two, and this difference involves the special *priority of the beautiful* (*einen eigentümlichen* Vorzug des Schönen). We have seen that the ungraspability (*Ungreifbarkeit*) of the good finds an analogue in the beautiful – i.e., in the measuredness (*Maßhaftigkeit*) of beings and the disclosure (*Offenbarkeit*) (*alêtheia*) that belongs to it – insofar as it finds a correspondence, in that it too has an ultimate effusiveness (*Überschwenglichkeit*). But Plato can say, moreover, that in the attempt to grasp the good itself, the good takes flight into the beautiful. Thus the beautiful is distinguished from the absolutely ungraspable good in that it can be grasped, it is part of its own nature to be something that is appearing (*Erscheinendes zu sein*). ... "beauty alone has this quality: that it is what is most radiant (*ekphanestaton*) and lovely." (TM, 496–97/GW 1, 484–85; trans. modif.)

The Form of the Beautiful thus plays a pivotal role in Gadamer's appropriation of Platonism. For being both a Form and "most appearing," it has the function of "mediating between idea and appearance." Stating that such is the *crux of Platonism*, he writes: "The idea of the beautiful is truly present (*wahrhaft anwesend*), whole and undivided (*ungeteilt und ganz*), in what is beautiful (TM, 497/GW1, 485)."

---

[41] Commentators usually refrain from reading the two passages together because allegedly *Republic* VI deals with the Good in itself and the *Philebus* with the human good – see e.g. Vogt (2019, 19) and Moss (2019, 234). Gadamer denies this premise (e.g. IG, 30).

Here again we encounter the idea of a participatory dynamic that emphasizes the mutuality or reciprocity between Forms and particulars: a beautiful being (*Seiende*) in its particularity does not merely "imitate" the Beautiful; rather, the Beautiful itself is present in it, "whole and undivided." But the presence of the Form of the Beautiful in beautiful beings is *not* the constant presence (*ständige Anwesenheit*) that Heidegger suspects and criticizes in Plato's *Ideenlehre*. With an oblique reference to the *Symposium*, where Diotima says that the sight of the Beautiful itself happens to the lover "all of a sudden" (ἐξαίφνης, 210e4, 212c6, 213c1). Gadamer indeed says: "It appears suddenly (*plötzlich*); and just as suddenly, without any transition (*ohne Übergänge*), immediately (*unvermittelt*), it disappears again" (TM, 497/GW1, 485; trans. modif.). The appearance of the beautiful thus has a distinctive, radically transient temporality. It has the "character of an event (*Ereignischarakter*)" (GW 1, 488, 490), and in this sense it anticipates the understanding of truth at play in hermeneutic ontology. Gadamer's emphasis on the *appearing* structure of the Beautiful recalls the Sun Analogy of the *Republic*, where truth is explicitly compared to *light* (*Resp.* 507e4–509a5).

In his appropriation of the appearing of the Beautiful and the metaphysics of light, Gadamer has been said to recover insights from Neoplatonic ontology as well as from the scholastic doctrine of the transcendentals.[42] Gadamer is indeed quite clear that the Neoplatonic tradition (as well as that of Christian mysticism) should be credited for allowing the Platonic understanding of beauty to reemerge and to be at the forefront. And he thinks of philosophical hermeneutics as being an integral part of that ongoing tradition:

> the Platonic view of beauty . . . is like an undercurrent (*Unterströmung*) in the history of Aristotelian and Scholastic metaphysics, sometimes rising to the surface (*zutage tritt*), as in Neoplatonic and Christian mysticism and in theological and philosophical spiritualism. It was in this tradition of Platonism that the conceptual vocabulary required for thought about the finitude of human life was developed. The continuity of this Platonic tradition is attested by the affinity between the Platonic theory of beauty and the idea of a universal hermeneutics. (TM, 502/ GW 1, 490; trans. mod.f.)

Gadamer indeed conceives of interpretation as a highlighting (*Überhellung*) by means of which the *interpretandum* is *brought to light, illuminated,* and so finds the Neoplatonic vocabulary of *illuminatio* (*Erleuchtung*) appropriate to capture the self-presenting (*Sichdarstellen*) of Being in language (GW 1, 119, 404, 488–89, 490–92). He also thinks of such self-presentation as an increase in

---

[42] For an emphasis on Neoplatonism, see especially Doyon (2023); for emphases on the transcendentals, see Wachterhauser (1999, 38, 86, 188) and Dostal (2022, 95–96).

Being (*Zuwachs an Sein*) analogous to the notion, central in Neoplatonism, of emanation (GW 1, 145, 427). That being said, Gadamer also quite clearly wishes to free these productive concepts from many if not most of their metaphysical underpinnings.[43] Notably, he thinks that Neoplatonism does not do justice to the historicity of human experience (cf. GW 1, 205–6). Most importantly, he thinks that it is possible to appropriate the Christian-Neoplatonic metaphysics of light while bracketing the question of the source of light – that is, the *theological* question of metaphysics: "the structure of light can obviously be detached from the Neoplatonic and Christian metaphysical representation of the at once sensible and intellectual source of light" (GW 1, 487/TM, 499; trans. modif.).

As for Gadamer's appropriation of the doctrine of the transcendentals, he also obviously thinks it is relevant insofar as it intimates a strong connection – what the scholastics referred to as the transcendentals' "convertibility" – between the Good, the Beautiful, and truth, a connection that is crucial in Gadamer's interpretation of Platonic Forms. Thus, he writes: "According to traditional metaphysics the being-true of of what is (*Wahrsein des Seienden*) is one of its transcendental qualities and is closely related to goodness (which again brings in beauty)" (GW 1, 490; TM, 502). Earlier in *Truth and Method*, he also praises the doctrine of the transcendentals for thinking of the relation between truth and Being as moments of Being itself as distinguished from a comportment of the thinking subject (GW 1, 462). However, just like in the case of the Neoplatonic *Lichtmetaphysik*, Gadamer wishes to appropriate these insights with considerable hermeneutic latitude. First, he thinks that the doctrine of the transcendentals can be freed "from its connection to the metaphysical doctrine of forma" (GW 1, 491/TM, 502). Second, *pulchrum* was not traditionally part of the transcendentals (which included *ens, unum, res, bonum, verum*),[44] but Gadamer proclaims the *Vorzug des Schönen*, the priority of the Beautiful.[45] Third, while the doctrine of the transcendentals is theologically oriented and points to truth as ultimately grounded in the *unchanging* mind of God, Gadamer thinks, as we have seen, that the Beautiful reveals the temporality of truth, which is for him after all an *event*.[46]

This is not to deny that Neoplatonic metaphysics as well as the medieval doctrine of the transcendentals and the question of their convertibility are

---

[43] See Grondin (2022, 33–35) and Doyon (2023, 190–91). This is compatible with Gadamer's claim that metaphysics remains a *possibility* so long as we actively *question* (GW 10, 108).

[44] With the exception of Bonaventure, as aptly noted by Doyon (2023, 188).

[45] Unsurprisingly, Gadamer thus disagrees with St. Thomas Aquinas on the question of beauty (GW 1, 490–91).

[46] See e.g. St. Thomas Aquinas, *Questiones Disputatae de Veritate*, q1a2. To say nothing of the fact that the scholastic account of truth is radically "orthotic": *veritas est adaequatio intellectus et rei*.

relevant to Gadamer's reading of Platonic Forms. He clearly *appropriates* these insight and frameworks, but he does so in such a way as to distance himself from their metaphysical implications. Most notably, he avoids the ontotheological (mis)construal of the question of Being (*Sein*) as the question of the highest being (*Seiende*) as well as the metaphysical determination of truth as correctness or correspondence.

Indeed, Gadamer's interpretation and appropriation of Platonic ontology not only responds to Heidegger's criticism of Plato, but also anticipates central Heideggerian insights. Identifying the Idea of the Good with the Being of Forms in general (*Sein der Ideen überhaupt*, GW 7, 198), Gadamer treats the question of the Good for Plato as the question of Being. Therefore, when he determines the Good essentially as self-withdrawal, Gadamer's Plato acknowledges *absence* and *hiddenness* as a defining moment of Being. To be sure, Being's self-withdrawal is the flipside of its appearing in the Beautiful, but this moment of presence is understood as ἐξαίφνης – that is, as the sudden and simultaneous coming to presence and disappearance. Thus interpreted, the Idea of the Good points neither to ontotheology, nor to a metaphysics of presence.[47]

Similarly, the present absence or absent presence of the Good through the Beautiful in the ἐξαίφνης points to Gadamer's understanding of truth as the event in which meaning shines forth and understanding occurs. Truth is not a correspondence but a sudden manifestness (*Offenbarkeit*) structurally akin to the appearance of the Beautiful: "the close relationship that exists between the shining forth (*Vorscheinen*) of the beautiful and the evidentness (das *Einleuchtende*) of the understandable is based on the metaphysics of light" (GW 1, 487/TM, 499, cf. GW 1, 488). Plato understands truth as this momentary disclosure, this temporal self-presentation – that is, as ἀλήθεια (GW 1, 484, 486, 491; GW 3, 243–44).[48]

A final point deserves our attention: Gadamer's interpretation of the highest summit of Platonic ontology brings us back to the concrete facticity of practical human life. It does so by emphasizing the importance of *measure* in beauty: "Harmonious proportion, symmetry, is the decisive condition of all being-beautiful" (TM, 495/GW 1, 483; trans. modif.). Likewise, he says that "Plato defines the Beautiful through measure, adequateness and proportionality" and "Aristotle states as the moments (*eidê*) of the Beautiful order (*taxis*), good proportionality (*summetria*) and definition (*hôrismenon*)" (TM, 495/GW 1,

---
[47] See EE, 170 where Gadamer is very explicit about this.
[48] However, Gadamer's treatment of Plato in *Wahrheit und Methode* is paradoxical: Gadamer's interpretation of the *Cratylus*' (GW 1, 409 ff.) points to a correspondence theory of truth, but his interpretation of the Beautiful and the Platonic metaphysics of light articulates an account of truth as temporal disclosedness.

482–83; trans. modif.). If this is so, and if, as Gadamer thinks, the event of meaning has the structure of the appearing or shining forth of the beautiful, then this means that some kind of measure is the condition of hermeneutic understanding and truth. But what measure is this? As understanding and truth always occur in and through language, we are entitled to think that measure must play a role in the speculative function of language. Borrowing once more from St. Thomas Aquinas, Gadamer understands this speculative function in the sense of *speculum*, which means "mirror" (GW 1, 469). Language is speculative in the sense that, in virtue of the mirroring-relation (*Spiegelverhältnis*) between word and thing, it has the capacity to *reflect* the thing and thereby disclose its Being (GW 1, 470).

But how can we "measure" our words to reflect and disclose what we wish to illuminate with them? Given the *event*ual character of truth and hermeneutic understanding, there cannot be a fixed, unchanging standard. The "right" word that is able to operate speculatively and disclose meaning will not always be the "right" word.[49] The measure cannot be absolute. Gadamer thusly recalls the features of the art of measurement in Plato's *Statesman*: "all that has to do with the measure, the fitting, the right moment or occasion and what is required" (GW 7, 197): τὸ μέτριον καὶ τὸ πρέπον καὶ τὸ καιρόν καὶ τὸ δέον (284e5). In the same breath, Gadamer claims: "one literally finds here the basic concepts of Aristotelian ethics" (GW 7, 197). What is needed to guide our linguistic hermeneutic experience is not an unchanging standard but a practical kind of wisdom attuned to the changing circumstances of our historical existences. The measure we need is nothing else than φρόνησις in the Aristotelian sense. Thus, Gadamer sees no tension between the rehabilitation of Aristotelian practical philosophy and the recovery of the Platonic metaphysics of light in *Truth and Method*. These two conceptual domains may seem sharply distinct from one another, but Gadamer ties them closely by emphasizing the mediating role of beauty and measure. As a literal translation of the title of his 1978 Element would indicate, Gadamer's interpretation of the Idea of the Good lies *between Plato and Aristotle*. The Platonic question of the Good points, *in fine*, to φρόνησις as the virtue proper to the practical embeddedness of human understanding – that is, to πρᾶξις.[50] And as Gadamer, following the early Heidegger, emphasizes the essential differences between φρόνησις and τέχνη, between ποίησις and πρᾶξις (GW 1, 320–29), his reading short-circuits in principle

---

[49] See especially Risser's (2002, 229).
[50] On the harmony of the Platonic Good and Aristotelian practical wisdom in Gadamer's interpretation, see Fruchon (1994, 333–98), Gonzalez (2018), Pageau-St-Hilaire (2019), and Renaud (2019).

Heidegger's criticism of the Platonic conception of Being as being-produced (*Hergestelltsein*).

4 Patočka's Negative Platonism

While best known for his work in phenomenology, Jan Patočka wrote significant contributions to the study of ancient philosophy, and especially Plato.[51] Yet as his major work on Plato – *Plato and Europe* – shows, his concern for Platonic philosophy is inseparable from his phenomenological concerns. This intertwining makes it almost impossible to read Patočka's Plato apart from his phenomenological thinking, and vice versa. Key to Patočka's phenomenology is his simultaneous appropriation of and departure from both Husserl and Heidegger.[52] My approach in what follows will respect this hermeneutic principle, although in a limited way, by considering Patočka's Platonism in light of Heidegger, and especially of Heidegger's critique of Platonism as metaphysics. As this is a somewhat novel attempt in the interpretation of Patočka, it should be able to shed new light on his Plato, as well as on Heidegger's narrative and the limits thereof.[53] More specifically, I shall show how in each of the three moments of his Platonism that I will discuss, Patočka articulates, sometimes obliquely and sometimes more explicitly, a critique of Heidegger. Section 4.1 addresses what Patočka calls "negative Platonism" as the proper way of approaching Plato after the "demise of metaphysics." In Section 4.2, I turn to the major theme of "care for the soul." Section 4.3 discusses Patočka's complex *récit* concerning the historical fate of Platonism in Europe in relation to Heidegger's competing narrative.

4.1 Negative Platonism

Written around the year 1953, "Negative Platonism" is not simply an interpretation of Plato. Patočka's aim there is much broader, as the subtitle of the essay indicates: "Reflections concerning the Rise, the Scope, and the Demise of Metaphysics – and Whether Philosophy Can Survive It." Central to his argument is the idea that Plato has a role to play both in the rise of metaphysics and in

---

[51] Apart from his work on Plato, Patočka published in 1964 a major study of Aristotle entitled *Aristotle, His Predecessors and His Heirs* [*Aristoteles, jeho předchůdci a dědicové*]. He also wrote on Democritus and Plato (1972–74).
[52] For a good discussion of this indebtedness and critique of Husserl and Heidegger, see Findlay (2002, 15–50) and Truhlar (2023).
[53] Patočka and Heidegger have often been compared, but there is not much scholarship that addresses his Platonism in light of Heidegger's critique of Plato. Derrida (1995) and Findlay (2002, 51–82) do contrast Patočka's Platonism and Heidegger, but not Heidegger's *reading of Plato*. Rare exceptions to this are Hopkins' (2011, 39) brief and passing remarks as well as Maggini (2016), who focuses solely on the question of Platonism and the fate of Europe (see Section 4.3).

philosophy's capacity to survive the alleged demise of metaphysics. But the very *question* of the death of metaphysics is already problematic for Patočka. Alluding to Nietzsche and the proclamation of the death of God, he writes:

> The air, as the great seismographer of the catastrophes to come said, is full of putrescence. Yet what is it that died? What is it that has been dismissed so thoroughly, once and for all, that only a monument erected by historians remains? *No one seems quite to know, because the question has yet to be posed adequately.* (NP, 175; my emphasis)

Much like Heidegger, Patočka is quite skeptical that such accusations and counter accusations mean that metaphysics has been overcome. In most intellectual landscapes, there is a broad and widely spread yet vague sense that metaphysics is "bad" and to be avoided at all cost, but that does not entail that it has effectively been overcome: "Do not many putatively antimetaphysical trends acknowledge and posit a metaphysics simply in virtue of the fact that and of the way they reject it?" (NP, 176). Metaphysics, Patočka decries, has been too often conflated with a "secularized theology" while it is in fact "much older than Christian theology" (NP, 178). Among the difficulties, he emphasizes that the histories of the early beginnings of philosophy in Greece usually produce a "reinterpretation of its origins from the standpoint of the newly constituted metaphysics." He then boldly declares: "thus we do not have a history of the genesis of metaphysics and are not likely to have one in the near future" (NP, 179). We may pause a moment to measure the implication of Patočka's twofold accusation: (1) we do not know what metaphysics is; (2) we do not know how it came about because (a) we do not know what it is and (b) we tend to misinterpret the beginnings of philosophical thinking in light of its subsequent developments. This means that Patočka thinks *Heidegger too* has failed to explain what metaphysics is and to trace its inception adequately. Naturally, Heidegger's method of phenomenological *Destruktion* is supposed to circumvent the difficulty of retrospective misinterpretations of the past, but if we take his claim seriously, Patočka must think that it did not successfully circumvent it. But what about Heidegger's identification of metaphysics with the understanding of Being as presence, with the understanding of truth as correctness, with the thinking of Being as ἰδέα, in short, with Platonism?

To say that Patočka simply disagrees with Heidegger would be misleading, for a single page later, he calls Plato the "creator of metaphysics" (NP, 180). Yet it would be equally mistaken to say that he agrees with Heidegger about the determination of metaphysics as Platonism, because Patočka thinks Plato plays a deeply ambivalent role in the history of metaphysics. On the one hand, Plato appears as a metaphysician: "The essence of metaphysics, as Plato, Aristotle, and Democritus formulated it, consists in offering an *answer* to the Socratic (or pre-Socratic) *question*" (NP, 181; my emphasis). On the other hand, Patočka thinks Plato is more rooted in Socratic questioning than Aristotle:

> Plato, the creator of metaphysics, remains rooted in this [Socrates'] premetaphysical soil and seeks to capture and exploit it by describing the figure of Socrates. Thanks to his towering philosophical and literary genius, he managed to create a figure whose symbolic significance vastly exceeds every historical reality, a figure that, with every reason, became a *symbol of philosophy as such*. Only a narrow-minded, lifeless interpretation in the tradition of Aristotelean logic (and *that* means *metaphysics*) could present this figure as a prototype of a deadening intellectualism that transforms *vital questions* into one of *logical consistency* and into an *art of correct definitions*. (NP, 180; my emphasis)

Such rootedness in the Socratic soil of philosophical questioning prevents Plato not only from transforming Socratic λόγος into propositional logic as "one of the three great disciplines of the new metaphysical philosophy" (NP, 181), but also from reinterpreting the "principle of Ideas and of the Platonic *eros* along cosmological lines" (182). Thus, Patočka implicitly revises Heidegger's diagnosis of the ontotheological constitution of metaphysics by locating its inception in Aristotle instead of Plato: "it is Aristotle, not Plato, in whom the project of metaphysical philosophy really, genuinely culminates In Aristotle, transcendence is transformed, with a fatal inevitability, into a transcendent, supramundane reality, a transcendent deity" (NP, 182).

This means that Patočka is not merely opposing an elenctic, aporetic (or early) Plato and a metaphysical (or mature) Plato who elaborates the "doctrine of Forms." The question is rather how to interpret Forms and to see whether they represent or not an "attempt to build a science of the absolute, objective, and positive whole" (NP, 182) or to "construct philosophy as a special scientific system" (BC, 3). Likewise, the mistake of metaphysics is not the transcendence of Ideas, but a specific construal of such transcendence. As a matter of fact, transcendence is a crucial point of Patočka's negative Platonism. Patočka thinks transcendence properly understood is intimately tied to the Socratic experience of freedom. Such experience

> is the experience of dissatisfaction with the given and the sensory, intensified by the growing awareness that the given and the sensory is neither all there is nor definitive. For that reason too, "negative" experiences are decisive for the experience of freedom, showing as they do that the content of passive experience is trivial, transient, and insubstantial. ... The experience of freedom is always an experience of the whole, one pertaining to the global meaning – without the experience of freedom the question of the overall

meaning of life, so to speak, lacks all significance. Socrates' dialectic was intended precisely to show that no sense object, no factual experience, can either pose or answer this question. For all these reasons we can designate the experience of freedom as one of transcendence. (NP, 193)

Equivocating once more on the role of Plato in the inception of metaphysics, Patočka attempts to distinguish the Socratic and Platonic understandings of the experience of freedom or of transcendence. To put it briefly, it seems that Plato transformed the experience of transcendence into Forms understood as transcendent entities, something Socrates did not do because he remained grounded in the fundamental insight of his knowing ignorance:

> The experience of freedom was the basis of metaphysics in its historical genesis and development. Socrates articulated this experience, using the idea of a *docta ignorantia*: he did not enter upon metaphysics itself. Only Plato did that ... Plato explained freedom as transcending the sensible and reaching the transcendent Being, a transcendence from the "apparent" to the "real". ... Here Plato presented the first adumbration of a positive (rationalistic) metaphysics. (NP, 195)

The ambivalence is patent: has Plato entered metaphysics or has he simply presented its "first adumbration"? Patočka never settles this question clearly. It rather looks like he sees this very ambiguity in Plato's work itself.[54] For Patočka, the proper interpretation of Forms resists seeing in the Idea an absolute object, or in fact any object at all. The experience of the transcendence of Forms is not the experience of transcendent objects, but the removal from any objectifying tendency whatsoever:

> The experience of freedom contains no vision, no final terminus, which our activity, ever object oriented, could grasp. The experience of freedom has no substrate, if by a substrate we understand some finite and positive content, some subject, some predicate, or some complex of predicates. It has the *negative character of a remove, of an overcoming of every objectivity*, every content, every conception, and every substrate. (NP, 196; my emphasis)

Yet Patočka thinks that Plato sees in Forms both objects and something different from, radically "other" than objectivity: "To be sure, the Idea as Plato describes it has *two aspects*. It is, undoubtedly, an absolute object, it is Form as such; but *more basically* than the seen, than the Form, it is *what enables us to see, to behold*" (NP, 199; my emphasis). This "power of the Idea" to enable the seeing of objects cannot itself be something "objective" and that can itself be seen: "far from being the object-in-itself, it is only the origin and wellspring of all *human* objectification – though only because it is first and more basically the

---

[54] Truhlar (2023, 116) notes this ambivalence too.

power of deobjectification and derealization" (199). One of the great originalities of Patočka's interpretation of Plato is to see this deobjectifying power of the Ideas in the thesis of their separation (χωρισμός). The χωρισμός, he says, "is an important phenomenon that we cannot ignore and silence." It does not point to a realm of higher objects but to separateness or distance itself:

> *Chorismos* meant originally a separateness without a second object realm. ...
> It does not entail the secret of another continent, somewhere beyond
> a separating ocean ... the mystery of the *chorismos* is like the experience
> of freedom, an experience of a *distance with respect to real things, of
> a meaning independent of the objective and the sensory which we reach by
> inverting the original, "natural" orientation of life.* (NP, 198; my emphasis)

Therefore, on Patočka's reading, the Platonic χωρισμός is not metaphysics, but the expression of the radical freedom characteristic of Socrates' ability to distance himself from the given. It is, mutatis mutandis, very much like the phenomenological ἐποχή, namely the bracketing of what we normally accept and are captivated by.[55] Patočka acknowledges that such a resistance to the luring power of the world as we naturally experience it represents a tremendous task for us finite human beings. This is why he calls the Idea not just transcendence but the "call of transcendence," a call whose genuine answering is an "ever-repeated effort." In other words, negative Platonism is not just negative in that it negates the objectifying tendencies of metaphysics, but also in that it reveals the "limits [we] cannot transcend" (NP, 205). In light of the call of transcendence, we humans stand between the descending movement that weighs us back toward the given and the ascending movement away from the given. The Platonic Idea

> is not an object of contemplation because it is not an object at all. It is
> essential to understanding human life, its experience of freedom, its inner
> historicity. It comes to us and proves itself a constant call to go beyond mere
> objectivity, mere factuality whose outward presupposition is the human
> creation of novelty and *our ever-repeated effort to break free of the decay
> to which we are condemned by dwelling solely within the given.* (NP, 204; my
> emphasis)

Patočka's language here evokes Heidegger's distinction between authentic existence and inauthentic fallenness, which will importantly play out in the Czech thinker's account of Platonic care for the soul. Before considering how

---

[55] Patočka thinks that phenomenology "is always present in philosophy" (BC, 4), and, in *Plato and Europe*, he explicitly connects Socratic inquiry with the phenomenological ἐποχή (PE, 92). On this point, see also Ulmann (2011, 78–79).

Patočka's understanding of care for the soul anticipates several important Heideggerian insights, it is worth noting how his articulation of a negative Platonism already responds to Heidegger's attack against Platonism as metaphysics. The negative interpretation of Platonic Forms opposes the traditional "substantialist" interpretation: "the Idea cannot be a hierarchical system of substances, essences, *ousia*" and it "is not a species or a genus, as the metaphysical versions would have it" (NP, 200). Since the Idea is no object or "super-object" according to Patočka, it cannot be led back to an understanding of being as the presence-at-hand (*Vorhandenheit*) of present-at-hand entities (*das Vorhandene*). Likewise, it does not betray an understanding of being as producedness (*Hergestelltsein*), for there is according to Patočka's negative Platonism no demiurgic production of Ideas. Relatedly, and as we have already seen, the Idea as a deobjectifying power requires us to think of transcendence as radically different from transcendent beings or a transcendent being (*Seiende*). Negatively understood, then, Platonic Ideas do not point to an understanding of Being (*Sein*) in terms of a supreme being (*Seiende*): it does not fall into the broad ontotheological structure of metaphysics decried by Heidegger. As I have shown in my presentation of Heidegger's Plato, the metaphysics of presence is not only latent in producedness and presence-at-hand (*Vorhandenheit*), but also and very importantly in the presence (*Anwesenheit*) for the sight of a beholder. This in turn points, according to Heidegger, to the contemplative subject as the site of truth and so to a metaphysics of subjectivity.

I see three potential rejoinders to this worry in Patočka. First, the Idea, being no object at all, *cannot be seen*: it allows entities to be seen, but it does so only insofar as it is no object (NP, 199). Second, negative Platonism deobjectifies the Idea without falling back into the opposite pole of subjectivity: "if stripped of metaphysical encrustations," the Idea "stands above both subjective and objective existents" (NP, 200). But is not the experience of freedom so central to Patočka's Platonism a subjective experience? Yes and no. It surely is a human experience, which, as lived out from the first-person perspective, is in a sense "subjective." At the same time, however, this experience is always the experience of a finite human being who is far removed from any mastering, self-sufficient subject such as it was construed by modern philosophers from Descartes to Husserl: "the experience of freedom, to be sure, takes place in man, man is its locus – but that does not mean that he is adequate to that experience." The third point is related to this experience of freedom, of Socrates's radical questioning: Socrates' "knowledge is characterized as the learned ignorance, that is, *as a question*. Socrates is the great questioner. Only as a great questioner is he the grand contestant in dialectical discussions whom Plato describes. He could not be that masterful contestant if he were not wholly free" (NP, 180; my emphasis).⁵⁶ Here Patočka's negative Platonism resonates with the priority of Socratic questioning at the heart of the Platonism of Strauss and Gadamer. As I discussed earlier in Section 2.2, the being of a question is not that of constant presence (*ständige Anwesenheit*). Even though in *Plato and Europe*, Patočka does speak of "what endures in constant presence" as the "philosophical motif" of Socratic questioning (PE, 84), no other genuine presence is reached through that inquiry besides the persistence, the enduring presence *of the questioning itself* over and against the fleeting character of unexamined opinions and the too eagerly accepted given.⁵⁷ As I have pointed out in my discussion of Strauss' zetetic Platonism, there are great affinities between this insistence on Socratic questioning and Heidegger's own emphasis on the primacy of questions over answers in philosophy.⁵⁸ And Patočka himself acknowledged implicitly this affinity by characterizing Heidegger, *just like Socrates*, as a radical questioner: "No one in our age was able to ask questions so unrelentingly, so penetratingly, so exhaustively, as Heidegger" (HT, 14).⁵⁹ The difference, of course, is that Heidegger thinks of Platonism as forfeiting questions for erroneous and doctrinal answers. But Patočka's effort in his negative Platonism is precisely to strip Platonism (or the Platonic tradition) of such answers to recover its rootedness in the "premetaphysical soil" of Socratism. In this sense, negative Platonism as a "nonmetaphsyical interpretation" does not simply reject metaphysics but attempts to "'transcend and preserve' (*aufheben*)" it by recovering its original questioning sources (NP, 197).⁶⁰ If Plato can be read negatively, Heidegger's intention to "overcome Platonism" (cf. GA 65, 221) is in an important sense supererogatory. Let us now examine how this negative, purified, finite Platonism is compatible with the central motif of Patočka's Plato care for the soul.

4.2 Care for the Soul

In "Eternity and Historicity," a posthumously published essay written around the same years as "Negative Platonism," Patočka wrote: "Philosophy as care for the soul is the Socratic answer to the Socratic question."⁶¹ As we have seen, Patočka claimed that the inception of metaphysics was due to an answering of the Socratic question. The question we must now raise is whether "care for the soul" as the Socratic answer to the Socratic question avoids the pitfalls of dogmatic metaphysics, and if so, how. As Findlay argued, there is prima facie

---

⁵⁶ See also Učník (2016, 166–68).
⁵⁷ Patočka elsewhere compares the prisoners' situation in Plato's cave with what phenomenology calls the "natural attitude" (CP, 296).
⁵⁸ See also Dodd (2023, 138–39).   ⁵⁹ See also Findlay (2002, 49).
⁶⁰ See also Arnason (2007, 21) and Dodd (2023, 135–36).   ⁶¹ Cited in Findlay (2002, 78).

a paradox in adopting a nonmetaphysical Platonism and in appropriating putatively metaphysical concepts such as the notion of the soul. This problem is intensified when we hear Patočka saying: "I believe that Plato's entire philosophy is in its nature, in its substance a doctrine of the ψυχή (soul)" (SP, 81). Findlay thinks we ought to distinguish between a use of metaphysical concepts and a use of metaphysical symbols or metaphors.[62] While Findlay is right that Patočka's emphasis on the Platonic soul should not be read as a fallback onto metaphysical doctrines, the fact is that Patočka does not call the soul a symbol or a metaphor. He does talk about the Platonic images of the soul's upward and downward movements as metaphors, but he immediately qualifies his statements and claims that they are "not mere metaphors" and perhaps "something more": "These metaphors are not mere metaphors, but perhaps they are the most fundamental experience of movement man is capable of at all" (PE, 197–98, cf. 41).

The movement of the soul is then more than a metaphor, and the soul *itself* need not be conceived as a metaphor. In other words, Patočka does not deny the existence and reality of the soul. Just like in the case of the χωρισμός, his point is rather to reinterpret the notion in a new way.[63] Let us then consider how he defines the soul. In *Plato and Europe*, Patočka says that "the soul is that which is capable of truth," namely "that to which things are revealed as they are, or that and what they are" (PE, 38). Later in the lectures, he claims that the soul "is the center that mediates between being as the foundation of all existence, between principal being and the weakened being of things around us" (PE, 109). There is an unmistakable resemblance between these definitions of the soul and Heidegger's account of Dasein as the site of truth and as mediating between beings (*Seiende*) and Being (*Sein*). In that respect, Patočka can embrace the Platonic notion of the soul without being committed either to a metaphysics of subjectivity or to a metaphysics of substance: ψυχή disavows neither Heidegger's step beyond the subject–object opposition nor his critique of traditional substance metaphysics.[64] Of course, what the soul is for Patočka is inseparable from the notion of care for the soul: "The soul is just what is capable of taking care of itself" (PE, 106). We shall now see that his account of care for the soul is once more very close to Heidegger's analysis of Dasein. Key to this account is another characterization of the soul as "what is movable," "that

---

[62] Findlay (2002, 62).   [63] See also Dodd (2023, 145).
[64] Patočka points out that Heidegger sees an important filiation between Dasein or existence in his sense and ψυχή in the Platonic-Aristotelian sense (CP, 314) and quotes Heidegger (GA 24, 103): "Die Richtung auf das Subjekt bzw. auf das, was im Grunde damit gemeint ist, unser Dasein, nimmt auch schon die noch gar nicht subjektivistisch im neuzeitlichen Sinne orientierte ontologische Fragestellung der Antike, die des Plato und Aristoteles."

which moves itself," or "the principle of movement" (PE, 109; SP, 80; PE, 126; *Phdr.* 245c–e; *Leg.* 895e10–896a2), for Patočka thinks of care for the soul essentially in terms of movement.[65]

Although he claims that the idea of care for the soul is there in Democritus, the very words ἐπιμελεῖσθαι τῆς ψυχῆς occur in Plato's dialogues (*Apol.* 30b1–2, cf. *Alc. I* 132c1; PE, 77). Care for the soul is the center of gravity of Platonic thinking, Patočka claims. It is so pervasive because it is a very broad phenomenon, indeed a threefold movement: "care of the soul manifests itself in three ways: in one way as the complete plan of existence, in another as the plan of a new political life, and in yet another as the clarification of what the soul is in itself" (PE, 86) The "three currents" of care for the soul are (1) ontocosmological care for the soul, (2) care for the soul in the city, and (3) care for the soul "regarding its inner life" (PE, 97).

1. Ontocosmological care for the soul is the "most distant" from "one's own core." Yet it is not an ontological or cosmological doctrine. Patočka rather calls it a "way of philosophizing" and a "*project*" (PE, 95). He presents it as an *inquiry* about the world and its origins, and stresses that Plato did not wish to establish its results in any fixed way:

> Plato never systematically presented this ontocosmological looking-in in any of his dialogues. What is most peculiar and most profound about it is that Plato did not write it down. Plato did not want to pass on this system as something completed and capable of becoming tradition. This is the forsightedness of a thinker who understands philosophy as a living work of someone who cares for the soul in thought and who avoids every final fixing of what he somehow advances, what he lays before us not just for acceptance or belief . . ., but rather for examination, for further work. (PE, 96)

Alluding to the γιγαντομαχία περὶ τῆς οὐσίας of the *Sophist*, Patočka calls ontocosmological care for the soul a discussion "intended as an honest battle about *what is*" (PE, 96–97). Drawing from the *Seventh Letter*, he also claims that Plato's refusal to pass down a cosmological system in writing is due to the fact that noetic insight (what Patočka calls "looking-in," *nahlédnutí*) exceeds λόγος and can be easily falsified when transposed into words. This risk of falsification is also why, he thinks, Plato did not write his teaching concerning the One and the indefinite Dyad as the two fundamental principles of ontology. Like Gadamer, Patočka follows Jacob Klein in arguing that this mathematical structure is crucial to Plato's understanding of Being.[66] Also like Gadamer, he thinks that what is crucial with this twofold character of Being is that there is no

---

[65] On the soul as self-movement in Patočka, see Truhlar (2023, 57, cf. 117) but most importantly Karfík (2021, esp. 303–10).

[66] See Hopkins' (2011) very helpful paper on this topic.

ontotheological determination of the Dyad by the One, but rather a communal contribution of both principles in the constitution of any being. This he explains with a contrast between Plato and Aristotle:

> In Plato, we have the antithesis between the active principle, which is the One, and the second principle, which is the undetermined (the δυάς, duality). The first is the form, the second matter; form and matter are active: form unifies, material multiplies, divides, causes multiplicity. Both of them *are effective*. … In Aristotle material stopped being active, material is mere possibility, only the essential substrate for its forming. (PE, 192; cf. ADS, 51)

Forms, Patočka argues are "nothing but the first relations, *original relations*" between "*indeterminacy and unity*" (PE, 102). He goes on to claim that "ideas are numbers" (PE, 102, cf. 186, 210) but this he means in a quite specific sense: "they are not number one counts with" (PE, 186, cf. 100). For "only when variety is unified do we have something like a number before us, for type is something determined, something that has a certain form," and so numbers in the ordinary sense presuppose Ideas or Forms as "*archetypical forms*" (PE, 186). Platonic Forms are that thanks to which things we encounter appear as they do. They are, along with the soul that thinks them and with them, responsible for the appearing, the showing-up of the phenomena.[67]

2. Care for the soul in the city plays out as "*the conflict of two ways of life*" (PE, 97). It is the confrontation between the just person and the unjust person and is embodied in the conflict between Socrates and Athens. This political care for the soul is the only healthy root of the community: "because care of the soul is possible, the state is also possible, and the community is also possible" (PE, 121).[68] Caring for the soul in the city is the discovery of political responsibility as well as the active taking of such responsibility: "from the cultivating of our soul arises the possibility of forming the state, the community that is necessary so that a person like Socrates does not need to die" (PE, 121). Patočka's political engagement in Charter 77 testifies to his own commitment to this way of caring for the soul.

3. The third and perhaps most important current of care for the soul is internal or self-referential care for the soul: "the movement of the soul in its most proper sense of the word is precisely *care for its very self*" (PE, 124). In turning toward itself, the soul is turning toward a being that is immaterial, "not physical, not bodily, not a thing." The soul gets to know itself in reflexively examining the movement of its own thinking activity (PE, 124). In order to properly care for itself, to think itself, the soul must realize that it cannot rest satisfied with the

---

[67] See Hopkins (2011, 43–45).
[68] On the analogy between city and soul in Patočka, see Bernard (2017, 367–70) and Dodd (2023, 151).

material world: "This experience of the soul about it itself discovers at the same time that there exists a depth of being, which we unveil only when we swim against the natural current and against all general tendencies of our mind and all our instinctive equipment directed to reality, to materialness" (PE, 125). This movement away from materiality and perishability confronts the soul with the question of its own perishability, that is, with the question of its temporality and death. In a world in which "all things are somehow in decline, all are decaying, all are being worn out in time,"

> the impetus of the soul to discover what is precise, pure, and does not succumb to all these changes and oscillating is, at the same time, a battle against time. ... In relation to it itself, the soul is the discoverer of eternity. It tends toward eternity, and its most proper problem – the problem of the status of its own being – is the problem of the relation to eternity. (PE, 125)

It is important to emphasize that Patočka does not simply accept Plato's alleged doctrine of the immortality of the soul. Rather, he thinks Plato articulates a "myth of the immortal soul" (PE, 126). Because, he thinks, Socrates' arguments in the *Phaedo* "do not convince us and of course did not convince even the participants of that conversation," the question of the immortality of the soul can only find an answer in an "act of trust" (PE, 127). And since the Platonic myth of the immortal soul appeals to something like trust or πίστις Patočka claims that Plato is the first philosopher who transformed myth into religion. I will return to this bold claim and to some of its implications in Section 4.3. For our present purposes, the most important thing to note is that Plato's "religious" transformation of the question of the immortality of the soul is not for Patočka a way to foreclose the question of death by dogmatically answering it.[69] It is instead a way of caring for the soul by considering the question of its life and death. That the *question* of the soul's temporality and finitude has precedence over the alleged doctrinal proclamation of its eternity is quite clear in a text entitled "On the Origin and Meaning of the Thought of Immortality in Plato," which Patočka wrote in 1977, the last year of his life:

> Plato's doctrine of immortality thus is no solace to mortals who desire always more life and to always keep on living. It is a proposal (*Ansinnen*) to those who are capable of turning the alienation from life in this world into something positive, of living in the wonder (*Verwunderung*) and uncanniness (*Unheimlichkeit*) of ceaseless examination of that which is (*des ständigen Prüfens desjenigen, was ist*). (US, 111)[70]

---

[69] This resonates with Gadamer's thoughts on the matter – see notably ' Der Tod als Frage" and "Die Erfahrung des Todes" (GW 4, 151–72, 288–94).

[70] Jozef Majernik's translation (forthcoming) slightly modified.

Thus, the third current of care for the soul is intimately tied to a care for one's own death. In "On the Soul in Plato" ([2022] 1972), Patočka explicitly connected the notion of care for the soul with the *Phaedo*'s care for death (μελέτη θανάτου, 81a): "philosophy is defined here as an orientation toward death and even as a will to die; τῆς ψυχῆς ἐπιμελεῖσθαι can in this respect be understood as ἐπιτήδεια τοῦ ἀποθνῄσκειν καὶ τεθνάναι, the intention to die and to be dead" (SP, 79). The Czech philosopher interprets this care for death not as a comforting or numbing doctrine but, on the contrary, as something quite close to Heideggerian "resolution" (*Entschlossenheit*): "the Platonic philosopher, he says, overcame death not by fleeing from it by *facing up to it*" (HE, 105; my emphasis). Commenting on Patočka, Derrida was thus right to say that this Platonic "attentive anticipation of death, the care brought to bear upon dying" opens up the space "within which will be inscribed the *Sorge* ('care') in the sense Heidegger confers on it in *Being and Time*."[71]

Indeed, the Platonic care for the soul as appropriated by Patočka anticipates in various ways central Heideggerian positions. His interpretation of the soul as movement recalls the movedness (*Bewegtheit*) of Dasein that Heidegger emphasized on his path toward *Being and Time*.[72] His complementary definition of the soul as that which is capable of truth and the concomitant understanding of truth as revealedness or uncovering resonates with Heidegger's analysis of truth as rooted in the primordial disclosedness of Dasein itself.[73] Furthermore, Patočka's Plato, far from transforming the essence of truth into correctness, recognizes the "simultaneity of *uncovering and concealing*" (PE, 74) – that is, the mutual belonging of ἀλήθεια and λήθη upon which Heidegger insists: "concealing is also a kind of uncovering" (SP, 80). The further determination of the movement of the soul as care is also in tune with Heidegger's identification of *Sorge* as the structure of Dasein, and the emphasis on care for death, care *toward death* as the central core of care for the soul obviously evokes Heidegger's *Sein zum Tode*.

Patočka pictures care for the soul as a movement between two extreme psychic possibilities. In *docta ignorantia*, the soul knows its not-knowing. It is not satisfied with mere semblance and opinion, δόξα. At the same time, it

---

[71] Derrida (1995, 12–13) is also rightly perplexed by the fact that Heidegger does not quote or comment on care for death in the *Phaedo* (14). On "care" between Plato and Heidegger, see also Findlay (2002, 62–63). Hopkins (2011, 45) is right that we ought to avoid *reducing* care for the soul in Patočka to Heidegger's *Sorge*, but I am skeptical of his implicit view that the most important mode of care for the soul is its ontocosmological dimension: Patočka explicitly says that care for the soul's perishability is the care for the soul in the most proper sense (PE, 124) and that ontocosmological care for the soul is "most distant" from "one's own core" (PE, 95).

[72] See e.g. GA 61, 93, 114, 116–17, 120–30, 131–55, 160–61; GA 62, 308, 318, 320–21, 332–33, 349–62, 366, 368, 373, 385–85, 389, 395, 397, 404, 407.

[73] On truth as uncoveredness in Patočka, see e.g. US, 112 and PE, 30, 68, 150, 174.

knows that it does not know what is stable, permanent, ideal. "The care for the soul is, simultaneously then, the discovering of two fundamental *possibilities* of the soul" (PE, 93). In "On the Soul in Plato," Patočka describes this "twofold possibility of our being" as the oscillation between "fallenness" and "genuineness" (SP, 81–82). Genuine or authentic existence is a life devoted to truth, determinacy, and unity; fallenness is a state in which life is dissolved into semblance, disunity, self-delusion, and falsehood. Relating this oscillation to the allegory of the cave, he further connects these two extremes with ἀπαιδευσία (lack of education) and παιδεία (education) respectively, and claims that "education is possible only because the ψυχή (soul) is responsible for itself" (SP, 84). In this important sense, care for the soul is a matter of responsibility: "we are the authority of our own decline, we are responsible for our decline" (PE, 125). Patočka's emphasis on the idea that we are responsible for our own existence and our ability to live authentically or genuinely naturally echoes Heidegger's view that responsibility involves listening to the call of conscience and responding resolutely to it (e.g. SZ, 288).[74]

There is, however, a crucial difference between Heidegger's interpretation of the difference between regimes of authenticity and inauthenticity and Patočka's. As we have already emphasized in Sections 2.1 and 3.1, Heidegger's concern is purely ontological, and, because of that, the ontic content of Dasein's authentic or inauthentic existence is relegated to the status of a derivative and fairly unimportant question. However, just like Strauss and Gadamer, Patočka thinks we should not and indeed cannot abstract from the ethical-political texture of human facticity without doing violence to the human phenomena. He thus explicitly criticized Heidegger's fundamental ontology because "it doesn't find its way back to anthropology."[75] He also faulted Heidegger for not offering a "sufficient basis for a philosophy of man in community" and for insufficiently analyzing the significance of *Mitsein* (CP, 316; BC, 50). For Patočka indeed we cannot properly understand the being of human beings – Heidegger's "Dasein," which Patočka's Platonism simply refers to as "the soul" – apart from human embodiment, and we cannot understand embodied existence properly if we abstract from the ethical-social-political dimension of such embodiment. This is why, against Heidegger, he interprets care for the soul and authenticity in an ethical-political light.[76] This was already perceptible in the second "current" of care for the soul in *Plato and Europe*, namely political care for the soul, but it also quite clear in "On the Soul in Plato," where Patočka contends that

---

[74] As Derrida (1995, 15–16) suggested too.   [75] Cited in Findlay (2002, 39).
[76] Findlay (2002, 22) argues that Patočka sought to "apply" Heidegger's insights "to the social being of man," but I believe we should underscore the fact that this is no mere application or transposition: it involves a fundamental disagreement with Heidegger. On that specific disagreement, see also Karfík (2021, 317–18)

a responsible choice for a "way of life, βίος" is a decision in terms of "the order of values and imperatives of life," and that the most inauthentic βίος is that of the "tyrannical man, the man of extreme fallenness" (SP, 85; cf. PE, 217). Patočka's Platonism obliquely or implicitly suggests that there may have been a strong affinity between Heidegger's neglect of a properly ethical-political analysis of concrete human life and his personal involvement with the tyranny of the Third Reich.[77]

We may now return to the initial question posed in this section, namely whether Patočka's emphasis on and interpretation of care for the soul could avoid the pitfalls of dogmatic metaphysics as they are criticized by Heidegger and by Patočka himself in "Negative Platonism," and venture to answer it positively. Care for the soul is indeed *not* the kind of Platonism that Heidegger identifies with metaphysics. Rather, putting care for the soul at the heart of Plato's philosophy is a way of underscoring the *practical* matrix of the Platonic analysis of humans as temporal and finite beings. In picturing the soul as the site of truth as uncoveredness, as a movement toward its own self and as the injunction to confront its own death to live an authentic life away from our tendencies toward fallenness, Patočka's Platonism is closer to Heidegger than to Heidegger's critique of Platonism.

4.3 The Platonic Heritage of Europe

We may now turn to what is perhaps the most controversial of Patočka's theses concerning care for the soul. This daring thesis is that Europe has its very source and origin in Platonism, and specifically in Platonic care for the soul. According to Patočka, the decline and end of Europe is the consequence of its wandering away from this source and of the forgetfulness of its Platonic inception. With such an interpretation of the philosophical origins of Europe, he is at once quite close to and very critical of Heidegger's narrative concerning the history of Western philosophy and the forgetfulness of Being. Indeed, after summing up the three modes of care for the soul, Patočka cites Heidegger approvingly: "In all three of these directions, Plato's teaching is the grand metaphysic of the Western world. All metaphysics, says one contemporary thinker, is Platonism (PE, 127)."

As we have seen, there is in Heidegger's narrative on metaphysics as Platonism a crucial Nietzschean mediation. This mediation involves not just Nietzsche's own reversed Platonism as an avatar of Platonism and thus as the

---

[77] Compare what Patočka says about Socrates and tyranny: "Socrates, that man who several times showed that doing injustice is worse than sustaining injustice at the risk of his own life, stands firm during the rule of the tyrants" (PE, 85).

culmination of metaphysics, but also Heidegger's basic agreement with Nietzsche's critique of Christianity as "Platonism for the people." Patočka too agrees with this Nietzschean claim, although the specific and unorthodox way in which he agrees with it marks his difference with both Nietzsche and Heidegger. Let us consider this difference: "Usually it is said that European civilization rests on two pillars: one, the Judeo-Christian tradition, the other, antiquity. On my understanding, as I have tried to depict it, Europe stands on one pillar – and that is because *Europe is a looking-in [nahlédnutí]*, Europe is life founded upon seeing what is"(PE, 89–90).

Patočka argues that for Christian dogmatics and theology to develop, Christianity must undergo a process of demythologization accompanied by a requirement of self-justification. Both of these, as well as the thought of an "other," "pure" world of truth, goodness and divinity, are, he claims, of Platonic origin.

> So, in a certain sense, it is possible to say as Nietzsche did, although his meaning differs from my own, that Christianity is Platonism for the people. Nietzsche despises the basic thought Plato formulated, of some other world. And from this hatred of the beyond, he overlooks what is most fundamental about the phenomena of Socrates and Plato, that is, the care of the soul. (PE, 90)

Patočka thus agrees with Nietzsche and Heidegger that the Christian matrix of European developments is Platonic. But whereas Nietzsche criticizes Christianity's Platonism for devaluating life and Heidegger for its alleged ontotheological misunderstanding of the question of Being, he thinks that the Platonism inherent to the Christian tradition is rather healthy because it ties Europe to care for the soul.[78] But if Patočka can rightly claim that the *one* pillar of Europe is Platonic care for the soul, this means that Christianity is not merely a distortion of Platonism.[79] In turn, that implies that he accepts a broader and somewhat diluted account of what care for the soul means such that the history of Europe can be conceived of "as the history of care for the soul."[80] In the fourth of his *Heretical Essays*, he does indeed endorse a broader understanding of the notion than the one he articulates in *Plato and Europe*:

> The great turning point in the life of western Europe appears to be the sixteenth century. From that time on another motif comes to the fore, opposing the motif of the care of the soul and coming to dominate one area after another, politics, economics, faith, and science, transforming them in a new

---

[78] I thus disagree with Derrida about the putative "incorrigible Platonism" of Christianity in Patočka's interpretation.

[79] Although it is partly that due to its ontotheological interpretations of Platonic metaphysics (cf. HE, 107).

[80] These are Dodd's (2023, 162) apt words.

style. Not a care *for the soul*, the care to *be*, but rather the care to *have*, care for
the external world and its conquest, becomes the dominant concern. (HE, 83)

Naturally, the prioritization of having over being is a tendency that exists at all epochs – and Patočka does not deny that. Instead, he emphasizes that both original Platonism and its various later appropriations in Christian Europe acted explicitly against these tendencies to set the care to have over and above the care to be. This is obvious in Plato's dialogues and their recurrent critique of sophistry and rhetoric as ways of life rooted in the wrong presupposition that power and wealth are the greatest desiderata of human beings. (One can think of the first Book of Plato's *Republic* and the *Gorgias* as clear examples). It is also obvious in Christianity in a myriad of ways, from Christ's Sermon on the Mount (Mt, 5–7) to the various traditions of Christian asceticism. Thus, Patočka contends that the "Christian *motifs* of life" had "originally constrained this care to have, the will to rule" (HE, 83). One could indeed argue that the very spirit of *caritas* is antithetical to this pernicious care to have which, he claims, has now taken over Europe and brought it slowly but surely to its death. This triumph of the paradigm of possession and power – epitomized in Descartes' injunction to become *comme maîtres et posesseurs de la nature* (cf. HE, 84) – brings with it the acceptance of nearly anything that can contribute to the growth of having and ruling: such is the spirit of a technological society that has fully embraced calculative thinking as the only kind of thinking truly worthy of the name. With this critique of philosophical-scientific modernity, Patočka follows much of Heidegger's critique of modern metaphysics. However, it is important to note how he once more distances himself from the Heideggerian position. The most striking difference between the two narratives concerns the status of Platonism in the decline of European spirit.[81] For Heidegger, Platonism is *responsible for the decline*; for Patočka, it is the progressive overcoming of Platonism by the care for having and its concomitant instrumental rationality that is responsible for the decline. This has broader historical-philosophical implications: whereas in Heidegger, modernity is merely the completion or perfection (*Vollendung*) of antiquity and Platonism, for Patočka, we can hardly make sense of the decline of Europe without taking into account the revolutionary role of the modern turn.

It is difficult to pinpoint what exactly is Patočka's own response to this decline. According to Derrida, it would be to embrace a "full" Christianity "emancipated

---

[81] The other obvious important difference concerns their respective stances on the question of what we should do amidst a technological world. Patočka offers a somewhat "active" proposal where resistance, action, and hope are appropriate responses to the forgetfulness of care for the soul; Heidegger points in the direction of a serene letting-things-be (*Gelassenheit*).

from both Athens and Rome."[82] I think this is erroneous: Derrida's reading of Patočka's critique of Christian "Platonism" is a misreading. The "Platonism" that Patočka criticizes in Christianity is the ontotheological distortion of Platonism, a distortion for which Aristotle is most likely responsible (cf. HE, 109 and NP, 182). Christianity's original rootedness in the Platonic care for the soul and its enduring resistance to the triumph of the care to have are rather dimensions of Christian life that the Czech philosopher *praises* in his thoughts on the Christian tradition.[83] Is Patočka's solution essentially Christian? He does say that "by virtue of this foundation in the abysmal deepening of the soul, Christianity remains thus far the greatest, unsurpassed but also un-thought-through human outreach that enabled humans to struggle against decadence" (HE, 108). And when he explores the meaning of sacrifice as a potential response to the decadence of technological society, he emphasizes that the Christian religion differs from "those religions which conceived of the divine always as a power and a force, and of a sacrifice as the activity which places this power under an obligation" (DT, 339). Indeed, "radical sacrifice" is the fundamental modus operandi of the Christian God. Sacrifice might be a solution to leap beyond the domination of the care for having characteristic of the modern and postmodern ages. But it is quite clear that, unlike Dostoyevski, Patočka intends such sacrifice in a more secular, and perhaps even political sense – what he calls sometimes a "moral religion" (PE, 122, 127), sometimes a "demythologized Christianity" (DT, 339). At any rate, we are entitled to wonder whether this demythologization of Christianity can occur at all without the Platonic Socrates acting as its "fulcrum."[84] And so we wonder once more whether Patočka's project is not after all a kind of *Destruktion* of Christianity in order to retrieve and recover what he sees as its healthy roots: Platonic care for the soul. If this is the case, then Patočka's Platonic ventures accomplish or "complete" the original intentions of Heidegger's early *Destruktion* of the Greeks just as much as they turn Heidegger's more mature readings of Plato upside down.

5 Conclusion: Heidegger and the Plato Who Could Have Been

Eines muß ich Ihnen zugeben: die Struktur des platonischen Denkens is mir volkommen dunkel

Martin Heidegger to Georg Picht[85]

---

[82] Derrida (1995, 28–29). [83] See also Maggini (2016, 130).
[84] To use Dodd's (2023, 198) very apt imagery. For helpful reflections on demythologized Christianity and sacrifice, see Kohák (1989, 116) and Dodd (2023, 190, 196–98).
[85] Picht (1977, 203).

Recovering Plato after Heidegger's critique of Platonism is, as we have seen, the challenge that several students of Heidegger have taken up as their own philosophical task. Responding properly to this challenge demands that one articulates a critique of Heidegger's critique, or a *Destruktion* of his *Destruktion*. Such is the attempt of Leo Strauss, Hans-Georg Gadamer, and Jan Patočka, three thinkers whose works cease to look so different once we examine them in light of their Platonic inflexions. In my discussion of these three thinkers, I have shown how their Platonisms represent Platonic critiques of Heidegger. Their appropriations of Plato provide indeed compelling alternatives to both Heidegger's reading of Plato and the ensuing Heideggerian narrative concerning the declining history of Western metaphysics as a history of Platonism. For them, Plato does not teach any metaphysics of presence or ontotheological doctrine, but rather invites us to think relentlessly through the problematicity of Being from the phenomenological perspective of our concrete human, ethical-political facticity.

As we have seen, however, the Platonism of Strauss, Gadamer, and Patočka is at once critical of Heidegger's *Plato* and close to some of Heidegger's most important philosophical insights. This suggests that Heidegger *could* in principle have found a genuine ally in Plato had he read the dialogues differently. Heidegger seems to have been at least somewhat aware of that possibility. In the 1950s, he indeed wrote twice to Hannah Arendt to that effect. In 1951, he sent her a letter in which we read: "You mention Plato. I have him close at hand, but I need to get a few questions sorted out before I give myself the joy (*Freude*) of reading him once more and completely anew (*ganz neu zu lesen*)."[86] And in 1954, he told her that he would like to work out once more his own interpretations of Plato: "I would like to go through my Plato works once again, starting with the 'Sophist' of 1924/1925, and read Plato anew (*neu lesen*)."[87] Although Heidegger's confessed hope for a renewed, fresh dialogue with the Platonic dialogues remained unfulfilled, we do find here and there in the *Gesamtausgabe* passages that point in the direction of another Plato, a Plato who does not fit well into Heidegger's construal of Platonism as metaphysics and metaphysics as Platonism. By way of conclusion, let us look at some of these passages to offer glimpses of that Plato who could have been.[88]

We may begin with the most astonishing of such occurrences, which is a comment that stems from an observation on the *Phaedrus*. Found in the fourth lecture of *Grundsätze des Denkens* (1957), it reads thusly:

---

[86] Letter of April 1, 1951, in Arendt and Heidegger (2004, 125; 1999, 125; trans. modif.).
[87] Letter of October 10, 1954, in Arendt and Heidegger (2004, 122; 1999, 147–48).
[88] See also Gonzalez (2009, 263–64; 2015, 2019).

Through the dialogue between Socrates and his young friend Phaedrus, Plato himself speaks. He, the poetic master of the thinking word (*der dichtende Meister des denkenden Wortes*), speaks only of writing, but he at once indicates what struck him again and again, namely that, in thinking, what is thought does not let itself be expressed (*das Gedachte im Denken nicht aussagen läßt*). However, it would be hasty to conclude that what is thought is therefore unsayable (*unsagbar*). Rather, Plato knew this: that it is the task of thinking to bring the unsaid (*das Ungesagte*) closer to thinking and indeed as the matter to be thought (*als die zu denkende Sache*). Thus, even in his own writing we can never read immediately what Plato thought, although they are written dialogues, dialogues that we can only rarely release into the pure movement of collected thinking (*die wir nur selten in die reine Bewegung eines gesammelten Denkens befreien können*) because we are too eagerly and mistakenly looking for a doctrine (*weil wir zu gierig und irrig nach einer Lehre suchen*). (GA 79, 132–33; my translation)

These lines are astonishing for several reasons. First, Heidegger is suggesting that Platonic philosophy is close to what he calls poetic thinking (*dichtende Denken*). This would situate Plato in the privileged tradition of thinking poets and poetic thinkers such as Parmenides, Heraclitus, Anaximander, Hölderlin, Rilke, and Trakl, namely the rare figures in the Western tradition who seem to escape Heidegger's sharp criticism throughout his writings. Second, Heidegger here sees in Plato a deep awareness of the distinction between assertion (*Aussage*) and saying (*Sagen*), as well as an acknowledgment of the *limits* inherent to assertions and thus of any attempt to turn or transpose thinking into asserting (*aussagen*). If this is the case, then this new Plato could hardly be seen as the thinker who is responsible for the transformation of truth as disclosedness into truth as propositional or assertoric correctness. Third, Heidegger claims that Plato's meditation on the sayable (*sagbar*) as opposed to the assertable (*aussagbar*) leads him to conceive of the task of thinking as bringing the unsaid (*das Ungesagte*) closer to thinking. Accordingly, Heidegger's own *Auseinandersetzung* with great thinkers of the history of philosophy, understood as a hermeneutics of the unsaid, would be at least in some sense "Platonic." This is all the more intriguing given the fourth reason why this passage is so bewildering: we seldom succeed in approaching successfully the movement of thinking proper to Platonic dialogues because we are too eager to seek in them a teaching or a doctrine (*Lehre*).

There is a complex tension between the third and fourth points, for in the very text where Heidegger proclaimed "Plato's *Lehre* of truth," he claimed right at the beginning that "the 'doctrine' of a thinker is that which is unsaid in his saying (*das in seinem Sagen Ungesagte*)" (GA 9, 203). While in 1957, Heidegger opposes the thinking of the unsaid to the searching of a doctrine in

Plato's dialogues, the two tasks are conceived as identical in his 1940 "official" interpretation of Plato. Is Heidegger implicitly criticizing his previous reading? While we cannot definitely discard this hypothesis, evidences that he seriously revised his views concerning Platonic doctrines are very scarce, not to say absent. To be sure, by 1962, he seemed to have abandoned the view that the presencing (*Anwesen*) evoked by the Platonic metaphors of light should be understood as the presence of production, ποίησις (GA 14, 55). But the idea that thinking Being in terms of the Idea or Forms is to think Being in terms of a presence for sight, for a beholder, a thinking subject, seems to remain. The view that Plato's ontology betrays a metaphysics of presence is reasserted time and again after 1957 (e.g. GA 11, 147; GA 14, 84; GA 15, 333, 337); indeed, Heidegger states it only a couple of pages after criticizing the search for a doctrine in Platonic dialogues as a hasty mistake (GA 79, 143)! Thus, Heidegger's 1957 extraordinary intuition concerning the interpretation of Plato does not prevent him from proclaiming in 1964 that "metaphysics is Platonism" (GA 14, 71).

While Heidegger's understanding of Platonic philosophy as metaphysics is, as we have seen, already at play in the 1924–25, 1931–32, and 1933–34 lectures on the *Sophist*, the allegory of the cave, and the *Theaetetus*, it becomes increasingly rigidified in the second half of the 1930s through the *Beiträge* and the *Nietzsche* lectures. This process of rigidification culminates in the 1940 essay on "Plato's doctrine of truth." But upstream of this process of dogmatization, there are other hints of another quasi "non-metaphysical" Plato in Heidegger. In 1932, for instance, Heidegger devoted a whole seminar on the *Phaedrus* in which his analysis of the erotic condition of human existence came close to grant to Plato an awareness of the condition of Dasein as a striving toward Being (GA 83, 145, and 368). However, as Gonzalez has shown, such insights are short-lived and Heidegger's critique of Plato tend *in fine* to obscure them.[89] Similarly, in the 1930–31 seminar on Plato's *Parmenides*, Heidegger's discussion on the notion of the "sudden" (τὸ ἐξαίφνης, *das Plötzliche*) in the third deduction of the dialogue leads him to conclude: "The third way of the 'Parmenides' represents the deepest point to which Western metaphysics ever penetrated. It is the most radical advance into the problem of being and time."[90] But once more, this openness to another, strikingly different Plato, is quickly closed off by Heidegger himself.[91]

---

[89] Gonzalez (2015).
[90] From Marcuse's transcript of the seminar, cited in Gonzalez (2019, 329). See also Backman (2007).
[91] See Gonzalez (2019, 334–36).

Even in the 1920s, Heidegger had some insights into Platonic thinking that made Plato appear quite sympathetic to his own way of thinking. One of the oldest among such inklings is found at the end of the 1919–20 Freiburg *Grundprobleme der Phänomenologie* lectures. There, his appreciation of Platonic *eros* foreshadows some of the claims he makes in his 1932 seminar on the *Phaedrus*. Describing phenomenological philosophy as a movement between losing one's own self in life and coming back to its ultimate motives (*letzten Motive*) such as to allow a deepening of the self (*Vertiefung des Selbsts*), he claims: "The true philosophic attitude is in no way that of a logical tyrant who terrorizes life with his supervising gaze. Rather it is *Plato's* ἔρως" (GA 58, 263). How could Plato become for Heidegger the founder of metaphysics, if not precisely by divorcing Platonic thinking from the erotics of Socratic questioning? For if *eros* is, as Diotima pictures it in the *Symposium* (203b1–204b8), between Penia and Poros, in-between complete ignorance and the plenitude of knowledge, any account of Plato's philosophy as fundamentally erotic is incompatible with Heidegger's interpretations of Plato as championing reductive understandings of Being and thereby occluding the problematicity of the *Seinsfrage*. If Plato's philosophy is fundamentally erotic, this would mean that Being for him can only be "had" in the sense of *stiven for* and must remain the aspiring principle animating his intense *questioning*.[92]

As I have shown, this erotic and Socratic questioning is absolutely central to the Platonism of Strauss, Gadamer, and Patočka as well as to their Platonic critiques of Heidegger. We have seen that on this point of the primacy of questioning over answering, Heidegger and Socrates converge. This is probably why, in his brief course notes on Socrates from 1926, Heidegger appears quite admirative of Plato's master:

> Socrates: always, fundamentally and essentially attempting to achieve (*stoßen*) this knowledge, awakening (*wecken*) of an understanding of it, implanting an instinct for it. No new contends or domains, no new trend in philosophy. He left everything in its place, and yet he shook all things right to their foundations (*im Grunde erschüttert*): a new *possibility* and thereby a radical summons to knowledge and to the *grounding* of knowledge. Fact: no scientific results and yet a revolution of science ... Socrates was not a moralist who disdained the philosophy of nature. On the contrary, his concern was the *understanding of Dasein's knowledge and action in general*. He was no more concerned with determinate domains of the knowledge of nature than he was with ethical principles of delimited content or even with a special value system and its particular hierarchy of values.

---

[92] See GA 34, 204–18, Dostal (1997, 295), and Gonzalez (2009, 188–98).

> Socrates thought much too radically for such contingent matters to hold him fast. (GA 22, 92–93)

Had Heidegger not uprooted Plato from the Socratic soil of such intense, radical inquiring, students of Heidegger such as Strauss, Gadamer, and Patočka could have become much more "Heideggerian" then they ended up being. Yet as he performed a sharp scission between Socratic and Platonic philosophy and accused the latter of setting Western metaphysics on its allegedly catastrophic track, they had to criticize him to recover a more Socratic, less dogmatic, and more philosophically subtle Plato.

Abbreviations

Martin Heidegger

GA = *Gesamtausgabe*
SZ = *Sein und Zeit*

Leo Strauss

CM = *The City and Man*
GS = *Gesammelte Schriften*
HPP = *History of Political Philosophy* (ed. with J. Cropsey)
JPCM = *Jewish Philosophy and the Crisis of Modernity* (ed. K. H. Green)
NRH = *Natural Right and History*
ONIPPP = "On a New Interpretation of Plato's Political Philosophy"
OPS = *On Plato's Symposium*
OT = *On Tyranny*
PPH = *The Political Philosophy of Hobbes: Its Basis and Its Genesis*
RCPR = *The Rebirth of Classical Political Rationalism* (ed. T. Pangle)
WIPP = *What Is Political Philosophy? And Other Studies*

Hans-Georg Gadamer

CWM = "Correspondence concerning *Wahrheit und Methode*" (with Leo Strauss)
EE = *Das Erbe Europas*
GW = *Gesammelte Werke*
HG = "Heidegger and the Greeks"
HTJ = "Heideggers theologische Jugendschrift"
HW = *Heidegger's Ways*
IG = *The Idea of the Good in Platonic-Aristotelian Philosophy*
PDE = *Plato's Dialectical Ethics*
PP = "Plato as Portraitist"
PTI = Plato. Texte zur Ideenlehre
TM = *Truth and Method*

Jan Patočka

ADS = *Aristote, ses devanciers, ses successeurs*
BC = *Body, Community, Language, World*

CP = "Cartesianism and Phenomenology"
DP = "Démocrite et Platon, fondateurs de la métaphysique"
DT = "The Dangers of Technicization in Science according to E. Husserl and the Essence of Technology as Danger according to M. Heidegger (Varna Lecture)"
FP = "La fin de la philosophie est-elle possible?"
HE = *Heretical Essays*
HT = "Heroes of Our Time"
NP = "Negative Platonism"
PE = *Plato and Europe*
SP = "On the Soul in Plato"
US = "Vom Ursprung und Sinn des Unsterblichkeitsgedanken bei Plato"

Bibliography

Works by Martin Heidegger

Heidegger, Martin. 1975 [1927]. *Die Grundprobleme der Phänomenologie*. Frankfurt am Main: Vittorio Klostermann. (GA 24)

Heidegger, Martin. 1976. *Wegmarken*. Frankfurt am Main: Vittorio Klostermann. (GA 9)

Heidegger, Martin. 1977 [1914–70]. *Holzwege*. Frankfurt am Main: Vittorio Klostermann. (GA 5)

Heidegger, Martin. 1983 [1935, 1953]. *Einführung in die Metaphysik*. Frankfurt am Main: Vittorio Klostermann. (GA 40)

Heidegger, Martin. 1985 [1921–22]. *Phänomenologische Interpretationen zu Aristoteles*. Frankfurt am Main: Vittorio Klostermann. (GA 61)

Heidegger, Martin. 1986 [1951–75]. *Seminare*. Frankfurt am Main: Vittorio Klostermann. (GA 15)

Heidegger, Martin. 1989 [1936–38]. *Beiträge zur Philosophie (Vom Ereignis)*. Frankfurt am Main: Vittorio Klostermann. (GA 65)

Heidegger, Martin. 1991 [1929]. *Kant und das Problem der Metaphysik*. Frankfurt am Main: Vittorio Klostermann. (GA 3)

Heidegger, Martin. 1992 [1924–25]. *Platon: Sophistes*. Frankfurt am Main: Vittorio Klostermann. (GA 19)

Heidegger, Martin. 1992 [1942–43]. *Parmenides*, trans. R. Rojcewicz and A. Schuwer. Bloomington: Indiana University Press. (GA 54)

Heidegger, Martin. 1992 [1942–43]. *Parmenides. 2. Auflage*. Frankfurt am Main: Vittorio Klostermann. (GA 54)

Heidegger, Martin. 1993 [1919–20]. *Grundprobleme der Phänomenologie [1919/20]*. Frankfurt am Main: Vittorio Klostermann. (GA 58)

Heidegger, Martin. 1993 [1926]. *Grundbegriffe der antiken Philosophie*. Frankfurt am Main: Vittorio Klostermann. (GA 22)

Heidegger, Martin. 1994 [1947–59]. *Bremer und Freiburger Vorträge*. Frankfurt am Main: Vittorio Klostermann. (GA 79)

Heidegger, Martin. 1996 [1961]. *Nietzsche I*. Frankfurt am Main: Vittorio Klostermann. (GA 6.1)

Heidegger, Martin. 1997 [1924–25]. *Plato's Sophist*, trans. R. Rojcewicz and A. Schuwer. Bloomington: Indiana University Press. (GA 19)

Heidegger, Martin. 1997 [1939–46]. *Nietzsche II*. Frankfurt am Main: Vittorio Klostermann. (GA 6.2)

Heidegger, Martin. 1998 [1940]. "Plato's Doctrine of Truth", trans. T. Sheehan, in *Pathmarks*, ed. W. McNeil. Cambridge: Cambridge University Press, 155–82. (GA 9)

Heidegger, Martin. 2000 [1936–53]. *Vorträge und Aufsätze*. Frankfurt am Main: Vittorio Klostermann. (GA 7)

Heidegger, Martin. 2001 [1933–34]. *Sein und Wahrheit*. Frankfurt am Main: Vittorio Klostermann. (GA 36/37)

Heidegger, Martin. 2002 [1931–32]. *On the Essence of Truth: On Plato's Allegory of the Cave and Theaetetus*, trans. T. Sedler. New York: Continuum. (GA 34)

Heidegger, Martin. 2005 [1922]. *Phänomenologische Interpretationen ausgewählter Abhandlungen des Aristoteles zu Ontologie und Logik*. Frankfurt am Main: Vittorio Klostermann. (GA 62)

Heidegger, Martin. 2006 [1927]. *Sein und Zeit: Neunzehnte Auflage*. Tubingen: Max Niemeyer. (SZ)

Heidegger, Martin. 2006 [1955–57]. *Identität und Differenz*. Frankfurt am Main: Vittorio Klostermann. (GA 11)

Heidegger, Martin. 2007 [1969]. *Zur Sache des Denkens*. Frankfurt am Main: Vittorio Klostermann. (GA 14)

Heidegger, Martin. 2008 [1926]. *Basic Concepts of Ancient Philosophy*, trans. R. Rojcewicz. Bloomington: Indiana University Press. (GA 22)

Heidegger, Martin. 2008 [1927]. *Being and Time*, trans. J. Macquarrie and E. Robinson. New York: Harper & Row. (SZ)

Heidegger, Martin. 2010. *Being and Truth*, trans. G. Fried and R. Polt. Bloomington: Indiana University Press. (GA 36/37)

Heidegger, Martin. 2012 [1928–52] *Seminare: Platon – Aristoteles – Augustinus*. Frankfurt am Main: Vittorio Klostermann. (GA 83)

Karfík, Filip. 2021. "Jan Patočka on Plato's Conception of the Soul as Self-Motion," in K. Larsen and P. R. Gilbert (eds.), Phenomenological Interpretations of Ancient Philosophy. Leiden: Brill, 303–25.

Works by Hans-Georg Gadamer

Gadamer, Hans-Georg. 1978. *Plato: Texte zur Ideenlehre*. Frankfurt am Main: Vittorio Klostermann.

Gadamer, Hans-Georg. 1980 [1934–74]. *Dialogue and Dialectic: Eight Hermeneutical Studies on Plato*, trans. P. C. Smith. New Haven: Yale University Press.

Gadamer, Hans-Georg. 1983 [1931]. *Plato's Dialectical Ethics*, trans. P. C. Smith. New Haven: Yale University Press.

Gadamer, Hans-Georg. 1985–95. *Gesammelte Werke. Band 1–10*. Tubingen: Mohr Siebeck.

Gadamer, Hans-Georg. 1986 [1978] *The Idea of the Good in Platonic–Aristotelian Philosophy*, trans. P. C. Smith. New Haven: Yale University Press.

Gadamer, Hans-Georg. 1989. "Heideggers 'theologische' Jugendschrift," *Dilthey-Jahrbuch für Philosophie und Geschichte der Geisteswissenschaften* 6, 229–34.

Gadamer, Hans-Georg. 1990 [1989]. *Das Erbe Europas: Beiträge*. Frankfurt: Surhkamp.

Gadamer, Hans-Georg. 2000. "Plato as Portraitist," trans. J. Findling and S. Gabova, *Continental Philosophy Review* 33, 245–74.

Gadamer, Hans-Georg. 2014 [1960]. *Truth and Method*, trans. W. Glen-Doepel, J. Weinsheimer, and D. G. Marshall. London: Bloomsbury.

Gadamer, Hans-Georg. 1994 [1983]. *Heidegger's Ways*, trans. J. Stanley. Albany: State University of New York Press.

Gadamer, Hans-Georg 2022 [1990]. "Heidegger and the Greeks," trans. P. Vandevelde and A. Iyer, in P. Vandevelde and A. Iyer (eds.), *Art, Action and the Historical Dimension of Language: The Selected Writings of Hans-Georg Gadamer. Volume II*. London: Bloomsbury, 27–38.

Gadamer, Hans-Georg and Strauss, Leo. 1978 [1961]. "Correspondence concerning *Wahrheit und Methode*," *Independent Journal of Philosophy* 2, 5–12.

Works by Jan Patočka

Patočka, Jan. 1989 [1953]. "Negative Platonism: Reflections concerning the Rise, the Scope, and the Demise of Metaphysics – and Whether Philosophy Can Survive It," trans. E. Kohák, in E. Kohák (ed.), *Jan Patočka: Philosophy and Selected Writings*. Chicago: University of Chicago Press, 175–206.

Patočka, Jan. 1989 [1976]. "Cartesianism and Phenomenology," in E. Kohák (ed.), *Jan Patočka: Philosophy and Selected Writings*. Chicago: University of Chicago Press, 285–326.

Patočka, Jan. 2022 [1972]. "On the Soul in Plato," trans. J. Majerník, in E. Plunkett and I. Chvatík (eds.), *The Selected Writings of Jan Patočka: Care for the Soul*. London: Bloomsbury, 75–92.

Patočka, Jan. 1977. "Vom Ursprung und Sinn des Unsterblichkeitsgedanken bei Plato," in H. Pfeiffer (ed.), *Denken und Umdenken: Zu Werk und Wirkung von Werner Heisenberg*. Munich: Piper, 102–15.

Patočka, Jan. 2002 [1973]. *Plato and Europe*, trans. P. Lom. Stanford: Stanford University Press.

Patočka, Jan. 1998 [1968–69]. *Body, Community, Language, World*, trans. E. Kohák, ed. J. Dodd. Chicago: Open Court.

Patočka, Jan. 1996 [1990]. *Heretical Essays in the Philosophy of History*, trans. E. Kohák, ed. J. Dodd. Chicago: Open Court.

Patočka, Jan. 1981 [1976] "Heroes of Our Time," trans. P. Wilson, *International Journal of Politics* 11 (1), 10–15.

Patočka, Jan. 1983 [1974]. "La fin de la philosophie est-elle possible?," trans. E. Abrams, in J. Patočka, *Platon et l'Europe*. Lagrasse: Verdier, 239–63.

Patočka, Jan. 1983 [1972–74]. "Démocrite et Platon, Fondateurs de la Métaphysique," trans. E. Abrams, in J. Patočka, *Platon et l'Europe*. Lagrasse: Verdier, 265–80.

Patočka, Jan. 1989 [1973]. "The Dangers of Technicization in Science according to E. Husserl and the Essence of Technology as Danger according to M. Heidegger (Varna Lecture)," trans. E. Kohák, in E. Kohák (ed.), *Jan Patočka. Philosophy and Selected Writings*. Chicago: University of Chicago Press, 327–39.

Patočka, Jan. 2011 [1964]. *Aristote, ses devanciers, ses successeurs*, trans. E. Abrams. Paris: Vrin.

Works by Leo Strauss

Strauss, Leo and Klein, Jacob. 1997 [1970]. "A Giving of Accounts: Jacob Klein and Leo Strauss," in K. H. Green (ed.), *Jewish Philosophy and the Crisis of Modernity. Essays and Lectures by Leo Strauss*. Albany: State University of New York Press, 457–66.

Strauss, Leo. 1946. "On a New Interpretation of Plato's Political Philosophy," *Social Research* 13 (3), 326–67.

Strauss, Leo. 1963 [1936]. *The Political Philosophy of Hobbes: Its Basis and Its Genesis*, trans. E. M. Sinclair. Chicago: University of Chicago Press.

Strauss, Leo. 1965 [1953]. *Natural Right and History*. Chicago: University of Chicago Press.

Strauss, Leo. 1978 [1964]. *The City and Man*. Chicago: University of Chicago Press.

Strauss, Leo. 1988 [1959]. *What Is Political Philosophy? And Other Studies*. Chicago: University of Chicago Press.

Strauss, Leo. 1989. *The Rebirth of Classical Political Rationalism: Essays and Lectures by Leo Strauss*, ed. T. L. Pangle. Chicago: University of Chicago Press.

Strauss, Leo. 2003 [1959]. *On Plato's Symposium*, ed. S. Benardete. Chicago: University of Chicago Press.

Strauss, Leo. 2008 [2001]. *Gesammelte Schriften III*, ed. H. Meier and W. Meier. Stuttgart: Metzler.

Strauss, Leo. 2013 [1961]. *On Tyranny. Corrected and Expanded Edition including the Strauss-Kojève Correspondence*, ed. V. Gourevitch and M. S. Roth. Chicago: University of Chicago Press.

Other Works Cited

Arendt, Hannah and Heidegger, Martin. 1999. *Briefe 1925 bis 1975 und Andere Zeugnisse aus den Nachlässen Herausgegeben von Ursula Ludz*. Frankfurt am Main: Vittorio Klostermann.

Arendt, Hannah and Heidegger, Martin. 2004. *Letters 1925–1975*, ed. U. Ludz, trans. A. Shields. Orlando: Harcourt.

Arnason, Johann P. 2007. "The Idea of Negative Platonism: Jan Patočka's Critique and Recovery of Metaphysics," *Thesis Eleven* 90, 6–26.

Backman, Jussi. 2007. "All of a Sudden: Heidegger and Plato's *Parmenides*," *Epoché* 11 (2), 393–408.

Benardete, Seth. 2000. "Strauss on Plato," in S. Benardete, *The Argument of the Action*. Chicago: University of Chicago Press, 407–17.

Bernard, Marion. 2017. "Patočka et Platon: l'idée d'une politique de l'âme," *Revue de métaphysique et de morale* 95, 357–70.

Ciccarelli, Pierpaolo. 2018. *Leo Strauss tra Husserl e Heidegger: Filosofia pratica e fenomenologia*. Pisa: Edizioni ETS.

Ciccarelli, Pierpaolo. 2020. "On the Phenomenological 'Reactivation' or 'Repetition' of Plato's Dialogues by Leo Strauss," in V. Rees, A. Corrias, F. M. Crasta, L. Follesa, and G. Giglioni (eds.), *Platonism: Ficino to Foucault*. Leiden: Brill, 275–96.

Collins, Susan D. 2015. "Aristotle's Political Science, Common Sense, and the Socratic Tradition in *The City and Man*," in T. Burns (ed.), *Brill's Companion to Leo Strauss' Writings on Classical Political Thought*. Leiden: Brill, 441–72.

Crowell, Steven. 2013. *Normativity and Phenomenology in Husserl and Heidegger*. Cambridge: Cambridge University Press.

Dahlstrom, Daniel O. 2001. *Heidegger's Concept of Truth*. Cambridge: Cambridge University Press.

Derrida, Jacques. 1995. *The Gift of Death*, trans. D. Wills. Chicago: University of Chicago Press.

Dodd, James. 2023. *The Heresies of Jan Patočka: Phenomenology, History, and Politics*. Evanston: Northwestern University Press.

Dostal, Robert J. 1985. "Beyond Being: Heidegger's Plato," *Journal of the History of Philosophy* 23 (1), 71–98.

Dostal, Robert J. 1997. "Gadamer's Continuous Challenge: Heidegger's Plato Interpretation," in L. Hahn (ed.), *The Philosophy of Hans-Georg Gadamer*. Chicago: Open Court, 289–307.

Dostal, Robert J. 2022. *Gadamer's Hermeneutics: Between Phenomenology and Dialectic*. Evanston: Northwestern University Press.

Doyon, François. 2023. *Être et Vérité: Les origines platoniciennes de l'herméneutique de Hans-Georg Gadamer*. Paris: L'Harmattan.

Figal, Günter. 2000. "Refraining from Dialectic: Heidegger's Interpretation of Plato in the *Sophist* Lectures (1924/25)," in C. E. Scott and J. Sallis (eds.), *Interrogating the Tradition: Hermeneutics and the History of Philosophy*. Albany: State University of New York Press, 95–109.

Findlay, Edward F. 2002. *Caring for the Soul in a Postmodern Age: Politics and Phenomenology in the thought of Jan Patočka*. Albany: State University of New York Press.

Fried, Gregory. 2021. *Towards a Polemical Ethics: Between Heidegger and Plato*. Lanham: Rowman & Littlefield.

Fruchon, Pierre. 1994. *L'herméneutique de Gadamer: Platonisme et modernité*. Paris, Cerf.

Gonzalez, Francisco J. 2009. *Plato and Heidegger: A Question of Dialogue*. University Park: Pennsylvania State University Press.

Gonzalez, Francisco J. 2015. "'I have to live in Eros': Heidegger's 1932 Seminar on Plato's *Phaedrus*," *Epoché* 19 (2), 217–40.

Gonzalez, Francisco J. 2018. "The Aristotelian Reception of the Idea of the Good According to Heidegger and Gadamer," *Χώρα: Revue d'études anciennes et médiévales* 15, 611–28.

Gonzalez, Francisco J. 2019. "Shattering Presence: Being as Change, Time as the Sudden Instant in Heidegger's 1930–31 Seminar on Plato's *Parmenides*," *Journal of the History of Philosophy* 57 (2), 313–38.

Grondin, Jean. 2010. "Gadamer and the Tübingen School," in C. Gill and F. Renaud (eds.), *Hermeneutic Philosophy and Plato: Gadamer's Response to the Philebus*. Sankt Augustin: Academia Verlag, 139–56.

Grondin, Jean. 2022. "The Universality of Hermeneutic Understanding: The Strong, Somewhat Metaphysical Conclusion of Truth and Method," in T. George and G.-J. Van der Heiden (eds.), *The Gadamerian Mind*. London: Routledge, 24–36.

Hopkins, Burt C. 2011. "Patočka's Phenomenological Appropriation of Plato," in E. Abrams and I. Chvatík (eds.), *Jan Patočka and the Heritage of Phenomenology: Centenary Papers*. Dordrecht: Springer, 39–53.

Hyland, Drew. 1995. *Finitude and Transcendence in the Platonic Dialogues*. Albany: State University of New York Press.

Hyland, Drew. 2004. *Questioning Platonism: Continental Interpretations of Plato*. Albany: State University of New York Press.

Klein, Jacob. 1992 [1934–36]. *Greek Mathematical Thought and the Origin of Algebra*, trans. E. Rann. New York: Dover.

Kohák, Erazim. 1989. "Jan Patočka: A Philosophical Biography," in E. Kohák (ed.), *Jan Patočka: Philosophy and Selected Writings*. Chicago: University of Chicago Press, 1–135.

Lynch, Greg. 2013. "Limit and Unlimitedness in the Philebus: An Argument for the Gadamerian Reading," *Apeiron* 46 (1), 48–62.

Maggini, Golfo. 2016. "Martin Heidegger and Jan Patočka: Two Conflicting Paradigms on a Phenomenological Genealogy of Europe," *Balkan Journal of Philosophy* 8 (2), 123–34.

McManus, Denis. 2016. "On Being as a Whole and Being-a-Whole," in L. Braver (ed.), *Division III of Heidegger's Being and Time: The Unanswered Question of Being*. Cambridge, MA: MIT Press, 175–95.

Moss, Jessica. 2019. "Knowledge and Measurement: Philebus 55c–59d," in P. Dimas, R. Jones, and G. R. Lear (eds.), *Plato's Philebus: A Philosophical Discussion*. Oxford: Oxford University Press, 219–34.

Øverenget, Einar. 1996. "The Presence of Husserl's Theory of Wholes and Parts in Heidegger's Phenomenology." *Research in Phenomenology* 26 (1), 171–197. https://doi.org/10.1163/156916496X00094.

Pageau-St-Hilaire, Antoine. 2019. "Philosophy and Politics in Gadamer's Interpretation of Plato's *Republic*," *Etica&Politica/Ethics&Politics* 21 (3), 169–200.

Pageau-St-Hilaire, Antoine. 2024. "Too Radical Μέθεξις? Gadamer on Platonic Forms," *Epoché* 28 (2), 219–41.

Picht, Georg. 1977. "Die Macht des Denkens." In G. Neske (ed.), *Erinnerung an Martin Heidegger*. Pfullingen: Verlag Günther Neske, 197–205.

Prufer, Thomas. 1997. "A Thought or Two on Gadamer's Plato," in L. Hahn (ed.), *The Philosophy of Hans-Georg Gadamer*. Chicago: Open Court, 549–51.

Ralkowski, Mark. 2009. *Heidegger's Platonism*. New York: Continuum.

Renaud, François. 1999. *Die Resokratisierung Platons. Die platonische Hermeneutik Hans-Georg Gadamers*. Sankt Augustin: Academia Verlag.

Renaud, François. 2019. "Form and Language: Gadamer's Platonism" in A. Kim (ed.), *Brill's Companion to German Platonism*. Leiden: Brill, 349–78.

Risser, James. 2002. "Hermeneutics and the Appearing Word: Gadamer's Debt to Plato," *Studia Phaenomenologica II*, 215–29.

Rojcewicz, Richard. 2021. *Heidegger, Plato, Philosophy, Death: An Atmosphere of Mortality*. Lanham: Lexington.

Taminiaux, Jacques. 1991. "The Reappropriation of the Nicomachean Ethics: *Poiesis* and *Praxis* in the Articulation of Fundamental Ontology," in

Heidegger and the Project of Fundamental Ontology, ed. and trans. M. Gendre. Albany: State University of New York Press, 111–43.

Taminiaux, Jacques. 2002. *Sillages phénoménologiques: Auditeurs et lecteurs d'Heidegger*. Bruxelles: Ousia.

Taminiaux, Jacques. 2004. "Gadamer à l'écoute de Heidegger ou la fécondité d'un malentendu," in J.-C. Gens, P. Kontos, and P. Rodrigo (eds.), *Gadamer et les Grecs*. Paris: Vrin, 109–38.

Tanguay, Daniel. 2007. *Leo Strauss: An Intellectual Biography*, trans. C. Nadon. New Haven: Yale University Press.

Trabattoni, Franco. 2009. *Attualità di Platone: Studi sui rapporti fra Platone e Rorty, Heidegger, Gadamer, Derrida, Cassirer, Strauss, Nussbaum e Paci*. Milan: Vita e Pensario.

Truhlar, Dalibor. 2023. *Jan Patočka: Ein Sokrates Zwischen Husserl und Heidegger* (3. korrigierte Auflage). Wien: Sonderpublikation des Universtitätszentrums für Friedenforschung.

Učník, Lubica. 2016. *The Crisis of Meaning and the Life-World: Husserl, Heidegger, Arendt, Patočka*. Athens: Ohio University Press.

Ulmann, Tamás. 2011. "Negative Platonism and the Appearance-Problem," in E. Abrams and I. Chvatík (eds.), *Jan Patočka and the Heritage of Phenomenology: Centenary Papers*. Dordrecht: Springer, 71–86.

Velkley, Richard L. 2011. *Heidegger, Strauss and the Premises of Philosophy: On Original Forgetting*. Chicago: University of Chicago Press.

Vogt, Katja M. 2019. "Rethinking the Contest between Pleasure and Wisdom: Philebus 11a–14b," in P. Dimas, R. Jones, and G. R. Lear (eds.), *Plato's Philebus: A Philosophical Discussion*. Oxford: Oxford University Press, 17–33.

Volpi, Franco. 1995. "Dasein as Praxis: The Heideggerian Assimilation and the Radicalization of the Practical Philosophy of Aristotle," in C. Macann (ed.), *Critical Heidegger*. London: Routledge, 27–66.

Wachterhauser, Brice R. 1999. *Beyond Being: Gadamer's Post-Platonic Hermeneutical Ontology*. Evanston: Northwestern University Press.

Wrathall, Mark A. 2021 "Metaphysics (*Metaphysik*)," in M. A. Wrathall (ed.), *The Cambridge Heidegger Lexicon*. Cambridge: Cambridge University Press, 482–490.

Zuckert, Catherine H. 1996. *Postmodern Platos: Nietzsche, Heidegger, Strauss, Gadamer, Derrida*. Chicago: University of Chicago Press.

Acknowledgments

Work on this Element has been supported by a postdoctoral fellowship granted by the Fonds de Recherche du Québec – Société et Culture (FRQ-SC). I thank Daniel O. Dahlstrom and Filipo Casati for inviting me to contribute to the *Elements in the Philosophy of Martin Heidegger* Series. Thanks are also due to Jozef Majernik for encouraging me to study the thought of Jan Patočka and for reading a full first draft of this Element, and to an anonymous reviewer for providing helpful suggestions for its improvement. Above all and as ever, I am grateful to Ariane, Élie, Zoé, Joseph, and Anne-Marie for their continuous support and indefectible love.

Cambridge Elements

The Philosophy of Martin Heidegger

Series Editors
Filippo Casati
Lehigh University

Filippo Casati is an Assistant Professor at Lehigh University. He has published an array of articles in such venues as The British Journal for the History of Philosophy, Synthese, Logic et Analyse, Philosophia, Philosophy Compass and The European Journal of Philosophy. He is the author of Heidegger and the Contradiction of Being (Routledge) and, with Daniel O. Dahlstrom, he edited Heidegger on logic (Cambridge University Press).

Daniel O. Dahlstrom
Boston University

Daniel O. Dahlstrom, John R. Silber Professor of Philosophy at Boston University, has edited twenty volumes, translated Mendelssohn, Schiller, Hegel, Husserl, Heidegger, and Landmann-Kalischer, and authored Heidegger's Concept of Truth (2001), The Heidegger Dictionary (2013; second extensively expanded edition, 2023), Identity, Authenticity, and Humility (2017) and over 185 essays, principally on 18th-20th century German philosophy. With Filippo Casati, he edited Heidegger on Logic (Cambridge University Press).

About the Series

A continual source of inspiration and controversy, the work of Martin Heidegger challenges thinkers across traditions and has opened up previously unexplored dimensions of Western thinking. The Elements in this series critically examine the continuing impact and promise of a thinker who transformed early twentieth-century phenomenology, spawned existentialism, gave new life to hermeneutics, celebrated the truthfulness of art and poetry, uncovered the hidden meaning of language and being, warned of "forgetting" being, and exposed the ominously deep roots of the essence of modern technology in Western metaphysics. Concise and structured overviews of Heidegger's philosophy offer original and clarifying approaches to the major themes of Heidegger's work, with fresh and provocative perspectives on its significance for contemporary thinking and existence.

Cambridge Elements

The Philosophy of Martin Heidegger

Elements in the Series

Heidegger on Being Affected
Katherine Withy

Heidegger on Eastern/Asian Thought
Lin Ma

Heidegger on Thinking
Lee Braver

Heidegger's Concept of Science
Paul Goldberg

Heidegger on Poetic Thinking
Charles Bambach

Heidegger on Religion
Benjamin D. Crowe

Heidegger and Kierkegaard
George Pattison

Heidegger on Technology's Danger and Promise in the Age of AI
Iain D. Thomson

Heidegger On Presence
Richard Polt

Heidegger and the Elements of (Human) Being
S. Montgomery Ewegen

Heidegger and His Platonic Critics
Antoine Pageau-St-Hilaire

A full series listing is available at: www.cambridge.org/EPMH

For EU product safety concerns, contact us at Calle de José Abascal, 56–1°,
28003 Madrid, Spain or eugpsr@cambridge.org.

www.ingramcontent.com/pod-product-compliance
Ingram Content Group UK Ltd.
Pitfield, Milton Keynes, MK11 3LW, UK
UKHW020852180525
458533UK00014B/209